15-minute focus
Brief Counseling
Techniques that Work

SELF-HARM AND
SELF-INJURY
WHEN EMOTIONAL PAIN
BECOMES PHYSICAL

Funding to help underwrite the development of
the *15-Minute Focus* series has been generously provided by:

Maclellan Family Foundations

We partner with the courageous
to change the world.

....

PASTORAL INSTITUTE

SARAH T. BUTLER
CHILDREN'S CENTER
COLUMBUS, GEORGIA

The Sarah T. Butler Children's Center at the Pastoral Institute of Columbus, Georgia
is dedicated to the mental health and well-being of children ages 1-18. This center
provides comprehensive services that span psychological testing, intervention,
therapy groups, and counseling. In all our activities we seek to inspire growth
through faith, hope, and love.

Duplication and Copyright

No part of this publication may be reproduced, stored in a retrieval system, or transmitted in any form by
any means, electronic, mechanical, photocopy, video or audio recording, or otherwise without prior written
permission from the publisher, except for all worksheets and activities which may be reproduced for a specific
group or class. Reproduction for an entire school or school district is prohibited.

NATIONAL CENTER for
YOUTH ISSUES

P.O. Box 22185
Chattanooga, TN 37422-2185
423.899.5714 • 866.318.6294
fax: 423.899.4547 • www.ncyi.org

Print ISBN: 9781953945440 $15.95
E-book ISBN: 9781953945495
Library of Congress Control Number: 2021907122
© 2021 National Center for Youth Issues, Chattanooga, TN
All rights reserved.
Written by: Dr. Leigh Bagwell
Published by National Center for Youth Issues
Printed in the U.S.A. • March 2023

Third party links are accurate at the time of publication, but may change over time.

The information in this book is designed to provide helpful information on the subjects discussed and
is not intended to be used, nor should it be used, to diagnose or treat any mental health or medical
condition. For diagnosis or treatment of any mental health or medical issue, consult a licensed counselor,
psychologist, or physician. The publisher and author are not responsible for any specific mental or
physical health needs that may require medical supervision, and are not liable for any damages or
negative consequences from any treatment, action, application, or preparation, to any person reading or
following the information in this book. References are provided for informational purposes only and do not
constitute endorsement of any websites or other sources.

Contents

INTRODUCTION..3

CHAPTER 1
What Is Self-Harm or Self-Injury? 5

CHAPTER 2
Who Is Most at Risk for Engaging in NSSI?....................13

CHAPTER 3
What Is the Relationship Between NSSI and Suicidal Ideation? 19

CHAPTER 4
What Are Replacement Strategies?................................25

CHAPTER 5
How Can Teachers Help Students with NSSI? 31

CHAPTER 6
How Can School Counselors Help Students with NSSI?.......... 39

CHAPTER 7
How Can Administrators Help Students with NSSI? 51

CHAPTER 8
What Is Social Contagion? 59

CHAPTER 9
How Can Schools Partner with Parents
to Help Students Who Self-Harm? 65

CHAPTER 10
Where Can I Find Out More About NSSI?..........................71

RESOURCES...75

See page 75 for information about Downloadable Resources.

Introduction

I am not ashamed of my scars. I refuse to be. Most are discreet, but sometimes they get noticed. In the early years, when there were fresh ones in various states of healing, I would scoff when someone asked, "What happened?" My responses varied from the barely believable: "I was attacked by a cat" to "It's a long story." It frustrated me how many people seemed oblivious to the epidemic of self-harm. Are that many people truly ignorant, or is it just more comfortable to accept what is an obvious lie and move on? ~

– Margot

Self-harm

Self-injury

Self-abuse

Self-mutilation

It may be hard to imagine that someone would willingly choose to inflict pain upon themselves. It may be harder to imagine that they believe inflicting pain upon themselves actually makes them feel better.

For students who engage in self-injury, the physical pain their action creates pales in relation to the emotional pain they are experiencing. That is why they harm themselves. They are seeking relief. They are looking to escape. They want their body to bear the burden of their pain instead of their heart. The challenge is that the physical pain may bring some relief but it rarely lasts long.

Our students need our help. They need us to care about both their bodies and their hearts. They do not need us to agree with their choices to harm themselves; rather, they need us to understand their pain. In this book, we will discuss what behaviors are considered to be self-injurious. We will identify reasons why our students are engaging in self-harm. We will highlight approaches that we as educators can utilize to teach our students appropriate coping strategies, as well as interventions to address the root causes of their pain.

1 What Is Self-Harm or Self-Injury?

Self-Injury has been previously been known as self-harm or self-mutilation. As mental health professionals learned more about these behaviors, they have been more appropriately termed as Nonsuicidal Self-Injury (NSSI). This is a more accurate description of intention and purpose of these behaviors. NSSI is the act of directly and intentionally damaging one's own body tissue without suicidal intent and for purposes not aligned to cultural expectations or norms.

NSSI should be recognized as a maladaptive coping mechanism. Students often view the harmful behaviors as a coping strategy. Although there is potential for long-term injury, NSSI provides an immediate escape from overwhelming anxiety or stress. Students engage in self-harm to temporarily relieve themselves of intense negative emotions. They report that when they have strong uncomfortable feelings, NSSI lessens the emotional pain and brings feelings of calm and release. Whereas other students may express their emotions through tantrums, screaming, hurting others, and damaging property, students who engage in NSSI have learned to regulate those uncomfortable feelings by inflicting physical pain on their bodies.

Some students can become so overcome with troubling feelings that they often experience an emotional detachment. NSSI is a way for them to begin to "feel" something again. The physical pain serves as a catalyst for accessing the emotional pain that has become numb. Other students engage in NSSI as a form of self-punishment or anger toward themselves. Self-criticism and self-hatred are often at the root of these behaviors. Students feel as if they deserve to be punished. They are not good enough. Failure defines them rather than motivating them to learn and grow. NSSI is most often used in private as a way to quickly alleviate negative emotions; however, some students use NSSI to create a physical sign of their emotional distress for others to see. The resulting injuries are meant to communicate the depth of the pain they are experiencing. It is their cry for help when they cannot ask for support with words. NSSI can also give students a sense of control when they feel the world around them is out of control. This has been seen in some students who have experienced trauma. They engage in harmful behaviors in an attempt to "reenact" the trauma so they can resolve it in a different manner than they originally experienced.

NSSI or self-injury can take many forms such as:

- Carving in the skin
- Cutting the skin
- Subdermal skin abrasion
- Burning the skin
- Hitting or punching objects with the intention of causing bodily damage or injury
- Erasing skin
- Ice burning
- Biting
- Pinching
- Inserting objects under the skin
- Repeatedly picking at scabs to prevent healing
- Hair-pulling
- Head-banging (not associated with autism spectrum or other developmental disorders)

NSSI results in cuts, bruises, scratches, wounds, and scars. Cutting is the most common form of self-injury and is typically performed on the arms, hands, wrists, thighs, and stomach. The level of injury can vary from mild and superficial to permanent disfigurement. Studies have shown that when the behaviors result in serious injury, less than 7% actually seek treatment for their wounds.

There are three categories of those who self-injure: superficial, battery/light tissue damage, and chronic/high severity. Identifying the degree of use of self-harm helps to determine the appropriate intervention and treatment for the student. An assessment team, including a medical professional, will identify the level of NSSI in their final assessment.

Superficial

- Less than 11 episodes of self-injury

- Methods of self-injury tend to cause superficial damage, such as scratching, erasing, picking at wounds, hair pulling

- Typically use few methods of self-injury behaviors

- This is the least severe level of lethality; however, people falling in this class might be at an increased risk for suicidal ideation compared to students who do not self-injure.

Battery/Light Tissue Damage

- Less than 11 episodes of self-injury

- Methods of self-injury tend to cause light tissue damage, such as bruising, skin piercing, and small punctures

- Typically uses several methods of self-injury

- Students meeting these criteria are at a higher risk for suicidal ideation, a history of trauma, and disordered eating in comparison to the superficial class and those who do not self-injure.

Chronic/High Severity

- Higher frequency of self-injuring, greater than 11 episodes
- Methods of self-injury cause significant tissue damage, such as cutting, burning, and bone breaking
- Tend to use several forms over time (most serious form used results in high tissue damage)
- Students may have self-injury routines, report some degree of perceived dependence on self-injury, report hurting themselves more than intended, and report life interference as a result of their self-injury
- Students meeting these criteria are at the highest risk for suicidal ideation, a history of trauma, and disordered eating in comparison to other self-injury categories and non-self-injurers.

Students who engage regularly in NSSI do so in a cyclical manner. They may practice the injurious behaviors for a period of time, are able to stop, but will often resume the behaviors at a later time. This can make it more difficult to notice the physical signs of NSSI.

What Is *Not* NSSI?

Behaviors that do not result in immediate injury or damage to self, such as food depravation and excessive exercise, are not recognized as NSSI. These behaviors are better explained by another medical condition. Risky behaviors such as not wearing seatbelts, substance use, and engaging in dangerous activities where injury is possible (e.g., rock climbing, skydiving, extreme sports) are not considered NSSI. Body piercing, tattoos, and physical modifications that are generally recognized as religious, spiritual, or culturally acceptable behaviors are not included in the definition of NSSI. Students who engage in NSSI are not always experiencing suicidal ideation. In chapter 3, we will discuss in great detail the difference between NSSI and suicidal ideation.

When determining whether a student is engaging in NSSI, the most important consideration is not the specific method of injury; understanding the intention of the behavior is key to recognizing self-injurious actions. What separates NSSI behaviors is the intent or purpose of the behavior.

Dangers of NSSI

Self-injury and self-harm should always be taken seriously. Only 25 percent of students with a history of self-injurious behavior report only engaging in these behaviors once, but for many young people, one incident of NSSI may indicate a more serious issue, such as abuse or other mental health disorder (Whitlock, 2010). Studies have also shown that one self-harm event may be linked to increased participation in other risky behaviors. Even though NSSI is not a suicide attempt, students are more likely to consider and attempt suicide if they engage in self-injurious behaviors. Finally, most students who self-injure do not seek medical assistance for their injuries. Any evidence of NSSI should be addressed, especially if it is practiced regularly, using methods that can cause significant damage to the body.

Signs and Symptoms

Many who engage in NSSI work to hide evidence of their injuries from others, which makes the signs and symptoms of self-injury easy to miss. Those who self-injure most often do so on their arms, hands, and forearms opposite of their dominant hand (e.g., a right-handed person will typically injure their left hand and arm). Other areas used for self-injury are the stomach and thighs. These areas are easier to hide, especially from those in a school setting.

In addition to observing actual wounds and scars, there are other signs that a student may be engaging in NSSI, including:

- Dressing inappropriately for the season, such as consistently wearing long sleeves or pants in warm weather

- Constant use of wrist bands or coverings

- Refusal to participate in events or activities that require less body coverage, such as swimming or gym class

- Having frequent bandages

- Unexplained burns, cuts, scars, or other clusters of similar markings on the skin

- Possessing odd or unexplainable paraphernalia that could be used to injure themselves or clean a potential wound

- Frequent mention of self-injury in creative writing, artwork, journals, internet postings, emails, texts, or communication with others

- Changes in mood, including frequent irritability, hostility and anger, uncontrollable crying, or excessive sadness

- Frequent need for privacy and secretive behavior

- Unexplained withdrawal from activities or deterioration in academic performance and/or personal care

- Frequent high-risk behaviors that exceed normal adolescent behavior or a frequent disregard for personal safety

It is not uncommon for individuals who self-injure to offer explanations for scars or physical markings that may seem unlikely. For example, they may suggest that they were injured while playing with a cat. If the student is evasive or states that they are not engaging in NSSI, it is important to respect their right to privacy. However, if you have observed or continue to see multiple signs of potential self-injury, it is appropriate to share your concerns with a school counselor, school social worker, or school psychologist.

A Student's Story

It started earlier than I use to think. When I look back, I think I was maybe six or seven when I learned to use pain to help with pain. Physical pain, for me, was an easier thing to deal with than emotional pain. It slowly progressed with age. I started cutting at 14. I didn't know that self-harm was a thing. I did not know a single human who did it. When I looked back, and before I knew the neurobiology behind it, it was scary to me that a person's natural response to intense emotional suffering would be to cause physical pain. I was actively engaging in harming myself for five years. I used to count injuries, but I lost count after the first year. I tried to stop for other people, but at some point, I became addicted. ~ Alicia

1. Where did you learn to deal with your own feelings and emotions?

2. How do educators help students learn to manage their feelings?

3. Many students who engage in self-injury report feeling alone. How can educators ensure that all students feel connected to the school community?

KEY POINTS

- NSSI is the act of directly and intentionally damaging one's own body tissue without suicidal intent and for purposes not aligned to cultural expectations or norms.

- Students engage in self-harm to temporarily relieve themselves of intense negative emotions. Students also use the physical pain to access the emotional pain that has become numb. Other students engage in NSSI as a form of self-punishment or anger toward themselves.

- Methods of self-injury include cutting, burning, hitting, and interfering with wound healing.

- The signs that a student may be engaging in self-injury are subtle and the student may try to explain away injuries.

2 Who Is Most at Risk for Engaging in NSSI?

Recent research reveals that while approximately six percent of adults engage in NSSI, more than 17 percent of adolescents report using NSSI behaviors. More than 25 percent of those who reported use of NSSI indicated that they have had only one episode. Conversely, nearly seven percent report using NSSI on a regular and on-going basis and often utilize more than one method of NSSI (Swannell et. al, 2014).

The average age of onset for NSSI is during the early teen years, ages 12-15. Research has also identified late adolescence as a second age of onset (Peterson et al., 2008). However, there are some instances of elementary children as young as seven years old engaging in NSSI. Typically, these behaviors correlate with periods of transition. For example, early adolescents are moving from middle to high school. Older adolescents are experiencing a similar transition from high school to their postsecondary education and training. The shifting support systems, identity exploration, and finding their place in new environments can be particularly stressful and overwhelming for students. Likewise, when children experience significant events in their lives, they may be more at risk for NSSI behaviors if they do not have appropriate and effective coping skills and systems of support.

Both males and females appear to engage in NSSI at similar rates; however, the specific behaviors they use tend to differ. Males are more likely to use burning, hitting, and bruising, whereas females typically use cutting. Members of the LGBTQI community appear to engage in NSSI at higher rates. Although NSSI has been observed across various cultural and ethnic groups, there is a higher prevalence in Caucasians. NSSI has been observed in students across all socio-economic levels.

Experiencing trauma has been recently linked to NSSI. Emotional abuse by a parent, caregiver, or other significant adult is most strongly associated with NSSI. Interestingly, witnessing violence has a greater correlation to self-harm than actually experiencing direct forms of abuse. Similarly, when students feel heavily criticized or belittled, they are at a higher risk to engage in NSSI.

When students are experiencing the following, they may be at greater risk to engage in NSSI:

Increased amount of negative or unpleasant thoughts

- Poor communication skills
- Poor problem-solving skills
- Ongoing bullying and harassment
- Dysfunctional response to stress
- Physical, emotional, or sexual abuse, neglect or mistreatment
- Highly critical of oneself

Studies have found that one's initial experience with NSSI can be influenced by social contagion. Students have observed peers engage in self-harm or have been exposed to it through social media and the internet. Studies have linked identifying with alternative youth subcultures with a higher risk of engaging in NSSI. Additionally, there has been a significant increase in the presence of NSSI on the internet and social media platforms. This increase has been viewed as both beneficial and concerning. Exposure to acts of self-harm may trigger a student to engage in NSSI themselves. Conversely, one study found that over 33% of youth with a history of NSSI sought assistance and help through online sources (Transue & Whitlock, 2010). Although there is a connection between a student's first use of NSSI and social influences, repeated and on-going engagement in NSSI is associated with the student's perceived benefits of the self-injurious behaviors.

NSSI and Mental Health Disorders

NSSI often occurs within many psychiatric disorders such as borderline personality disorder (BPD), posttraumatic stress disorder (PTSD), depression, and eating and substance abuse disorders. The *Diagnostic and Statistical Manual of Mental Disorders* (DSM-5) included NSSI as a condition for further study, noting that these behaviors do not always occur within the presence of another diagnosed condition. Some of the proposed diagnostic criteria for NSSI Disorder include: repeated engagement in NSSI, belief that the NSSI will solve interpersonal problems, a preoccupation with NSSI, and significant dysfunction across several life areas as a result of the self-injurious behaviors (Gratz et al., 2015; Halicka & Kiejna, 2016).

Currently, NSSI has not been recognized as an addiction. However, self-harm does have some addictive characteristics similar to those of substance abuse. When students engage in self-injurious behaviors, they experience an increase of dopamine levels which elicits an increased sense of relief. As the student continues to engage in NSSI, the brain adjusts to the increased dopamine by actually lower dopamine production when the student is not self-harming, leaving them with a decreased feeling of well-being. To chase that sense of relief, students may increase the frequency of NSSI or engage in more harmful methods of self-harm.

Myths about NSSI

1. Only girls self-injure.	Approximately 30-40 percent of those who self-injure are males.
2. Self-injury is a failed suicide attempt.	Those who engage in self-harm are attempting to manage and cope with stress and negative emotions, not ending their life.
3. Only teenagers engage in self-injury.	The typical onset of self-injury is most common in early adolescents. However, documented cases of NSSI have been found in children as young as seven years old and it has been reported in adults as well.
4. People who self-injure should be put in a mental hospital.	For most people, self-injury is a coping strategy, just as drinking alcohol and smoking cigarettes are coping strategies. Hospitalization is not required for treatment or to help utilize more appropriate coping mechanisms.
5. Self-injury is attention-seeking.	Most people who engage in self-harm do so in very private ways. They work to hide any evidence of their injuries. Some people do utilize NSSI as a way to communicate their pain to others. If someone is harming themselves for attention, they are asking for help.
6. Self-injury cannot be treated.	Self-injury is a coping mechanism. If a person can replace the harmful coping strategies with another less dangerous one, they often stop hurting themselves. Additionally, the coping strategy is used to deal with distressing life events. Counseling can be an effective treatment for addressing these negative and/or painful circumstances. If the distress is related to a physiological condition, medication may be considered as part of the treatment plan.
7. Everyone who self-injures has a mental illness.	Self-injury has been reported as a symptom of several mental disorders such as borderline personality, depression, bi-polar, obsessive compulsive, and eating disorders. However, other recent research has recognized that some people who engage in self-injury have no other diagnosable condition.
8. Only people who are "gothic" or "emo" cut themselves.	People who engage in self-injury come from all groups, ethnicities, socioeconomic backgrounds, educational levels, and sexual identities. Some use self-injury as a way to function more effectively in their world. People who self-injure cannot be categorized by the way they look, their friend groups, or where they live.
9. Someone who self-injures can stop if they want to.	Some people who engage in self-harm can stop, but others experience a release of endorphins when they self-injure so the behavior becomes addictive. They need support to use more appropriate coping strategies.
10. I can't do anything to help someone that self-injures.	One of the best ways to support someone who self-harms is to listen to them with compassion and understanding. The painful acts represent an emotional pain. Creating a safe space without judgment can be very beneficial. Encourage someone who uses self-injury to speak to a counselor or therapist.

A Student's Story

I felt "abnormal." I felt like a failure.   I was twelve years old when I began hurting myself. I do not remember how I knew to cut my arms. All I knew was that it felt strangely good when I hurt myself. In my family, mental health issues were not recognized. There was no information on depression, eating disorders, or self-injury. All I felt was this overwhelming sense of shame. As a result, I tried to cover up my emotions and made up stories to explain the scar on my arm.

Things spiraled downwards in middle school. I attended a very competitive school, and everyone tried to be the best academically and physically. In particular, every girl I knew was dieting and was competing to see who could be the thinnest. It was like a plague and I could not escape it. I started to starve myself and would only eat an apple a day. But it didn't go as well as I planned. I started to binge on the weekend and I was not losing weight. I felt even more shameful and hopeless. I started to feel like that I had no self-control and I was letting myself go. Whenever I felt this way, I would pinch myself so hard that I couldn't feel anything anymore.

When my parents realized that I wasn't eating enough, they became extremely upset. So upset that my dad slapped my face when I refused to eat. All I remember was tears streaming down my face. However, I was told to keep quiet and make up stories when people asked about the marks on my face. Curiously, no one ever asked. It was as if everyone knew not to mention it. Instead, they alienated me and I fell into an even darker abyss. I contemplated suicide almost every day. I cried myself to sleep almost every night. ~Willow

QUESTIONS to CONSIDER

1. What are some of the developmental risk factors common to your students?

2. What information do you or your fellow educators need to know in order to be more aware of how your students may be suffering?

3. What supports does your school have in place to help students who may be struggling emotionally?

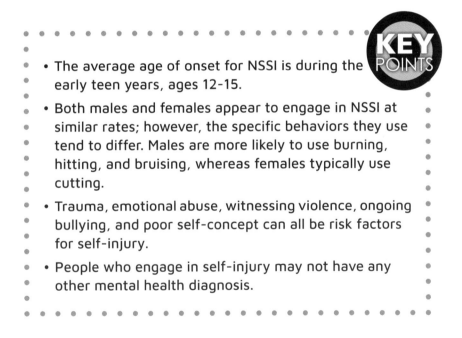

KEY POINTS

- The average age of onset for NSSI is during the early teen years, ages 12-15.

- Both males and females appear to engage in NSSI at similar rates; however, the specific behaviors they use tend to differ. Males are more likely to use burning, hitting, and bruising, whereas females typically use cutting.

- Trauma, emotional abuse, witnessing violence, ongoing bullying, and poor self-concept can all be risk factors for self-injury.

- People who engage in self-injury may not have any other mental health diagnosis.

What Is the Relationship Between NSSI and Suicidal Ideation?

3

Researchers have only been studying NSSI for the last few decades. Many early studies misidentified self-injurious behaviors as suicidal ideation. Both NSSI and suicidality involve behaviors meant to inflict physical harm to one's body, but more recent research has discovered that NSSI is separate from suicidality. Although these behaviors look alike, they are differentiated by the intent behind them.

People who engage in NSSI are attempting to cope or feel better. It is how they are managing their pain. Those who attempt and complete suicide want to stop their pain and try to escape feeling anything again by ending their life.

	NSSI	Suicidality
Intent	To transform emotional pain into physical pain; to preserve life but damage the body	To escape from mental pain and consciousness; to end life
Method Used	Cutting, scratching, hitting, carving	Shooting, drug overdose, hanging, etc.

Level of Lethality	Low levels of lethality; damage to skin or bruising; often not requiring significant medical intervention	High levels of lethality; damage to internal organs; significant medical intervention required to prevent death
Frequency	Regular or ongoing use when experience negative emotions	A single event; if suicide attempt fails, additional attempts are possible without medical and psychological intervention
Level of Psychological Pain	Emotional distress is increased; however, NSSI serves to manage or decrease pain.	Significant psychological pain and distress; unable to see a way to decrease pain except by ending life
Hopelessness	Low levels; NSSI is viewed as coping strategy.	Constant high levels; ending life seen as the only way to stop the pain
Consequences	Discomfort decreased	Completed suicide attempts results in death; attempted suicide increases discomfort

Although the *intent* behind NSSI and suicidal ideation is different, both behaviors do carry some of the same risk factors. These include:

- History of trauma, abuse, or chronic stress

- History of alcohol or substance abuse

- Lack of appropriate and healthy coping strategies for handling emotional stress

- Depression or anxiety

- Feelings of isolation

- Feelings of insignificance and unimportance

- Highly emotional

Engaging in self-injury can be a risk factor for suicidality. Up to 35 percent of people who use NSSI also report some suicidal ideation (Whitlock et al., 2015). These thoughts typically occur either at the same time or shortly after NSSI is practiced. Those who engage in more damaging forms of self-injury, such as cutting, carving, and burning, report more suicidal ideation than those who self-harm by scratching, punching, and pinching. People who engage in both NSSI and suicidal behaviors often have:

- More than 20 incidents of NSSI

- High levels of distress in the last 30 days

- History of sexual or emotional abuse

- Increased family conflict

- Poor relationships with parents

- Higher instances of substance abuse

- Increased feelings of hopelessness

- Increased impulsivity and risk-taking

- Diagnosis of major depressive disorder (MDD) or post-traumatic stress disorder (PTSD) (Whitlock et al., 2015).

Trained medical and mental health providers can help determine if a student is experience either NSSI or suicidality, or both. If a student is at-risk and displays any of the following warning signs, seek immediate professional evaluation and support:

- Talking about wanting to die

- Making a plan to kill themselves

- Feeling hopeless
- Feeling trapped
- Expressing that there is no way to end the pain
- Increased or regular substance abuse
- Feeling like a burden to others
- Anxiety or agitation
- Withdrawal from family and friends
- Extreme anger or rage
- Mood swings
- Too little or too much sleep

Support options for students wrestling with suicidal ideation or suicidal thoughts:

The **National Suicide Prevention Lifeline** is a 24-hour, toll-free, confidential suicide prevention hotline available to anyone in suicidal crisis or emotional distress. By dialing **1-800-273-TALK (8255)**, the call is routed to the nearest crisis center in a national network of more than 150 crisis centers. The Lifeline's national network of local crisis centers provide crisis counseling and mental health referrals day and night: http://www.suicidepreventionlifeline.org/

The **Crisis Text Line** serves young people in any type of crisis, providing them access to free, 24/7, emotional support and information they need via the medium they already use and trust: **TEXT 741741**: http://www.crisistextline.org/

The **Centers for Disease Control and Prevention** hosts a website on suicide injury and violence prevention, including research, publications, national statistics, prevention strategies, and resources: http://www.cdc.gov/violenceprevention/suicide/index.html

In her book, *15-Minute Focus: Suicide Prevention, Intervention and Postvention,* Dr. Melisa Marsh provides detailed information on strategies for implementing suicide prevention, intervention, and postvention programs, including ways to support students in a virtual environment.

https://15minutefocusseries.com/

A Student's Story

When I was in the seventh grade, I read a book about a young girl who had entered rehab for self-injury. I had never encountered self-injury before, but long story short, my young, impressionable, anxiety-ridden little mind thought it sounded like a good way to cope. Thus began my messy and painful journey for peace inside the hurricane of my mind. As I grew, things only got worse. I can remember countless nights of feeling like the sky was falling; my pillowcase soaked with salty tears. Self-injury seemed like the only way out. The only way to make my frantic mind quiet. To stop it from running in circles, from replaying every single thing that could go wrong. To be quite honest I didn't see the harm in it. It was an immediate release and it made me feel better. I wasn't trying to kill myself, so I remember thinking that it didn't "count." I thought I could stop. I would go months without it, but as soon as something bad happened, the cycle would repeat itself. This went on for five years. ~ Ari

QUESTIONS to CONSIDER

1. The intent of the behavior differentiates whether the student is self-injuring or attempting suicide. What are some factors you should consider when determining a student's intent?

2. Who are the mental health educators that serve your school? How do students access their services?

3. How can the adults at school collaborate to better support students?

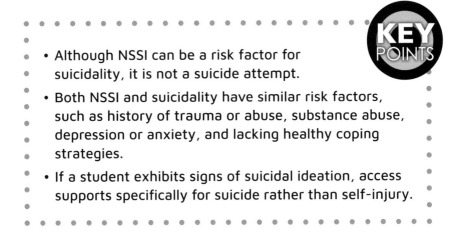

KEY POINTS

- Although NSSI can be a risk factor for suicidality, it is not a suicide attempt.
- Both NSSI and suicidality have similar risk factors, such as history of trauma or abuse, substance abuse, depression or anxiety, and lacking healthy coping strategies.
- If a student exhibits signs of suicidal ideation, access supports specifically for suicide rather than self-injury.

4 What Are Replacement Strategies?

Students engage in self-injurious behaviors as a means to cope with overwhelming negative feelings and distress. The best treatment will include counseling or therapy to address the underlying feelings that trigger one to self-injure. However, that process does take some time, so it is important for students who use NSSI to have an alternate and safe coping strategy they can use during that process.

Replacement strategies are behaviors and actions that students can employ instead of NSSIs. These coping mechanisms encourage the student to respond differently when they feel like cutting or hurting themselves. Replacement strategies can help the student express emotions without causing physical damage to the body. These strategies involve less risk of injury and can help the student engage in more productive behaviors. Research has found that if a person can delay engaging in self-injury when they first feel the desire, even for just a few minutes, the urge to harm themselves may pass (Kilburn & Whitlock, 2009). Replacement strategies can help to delay engaging in injurious behaviors. People around the student who self-injures can support them by encouraging the use of replacement strategies. If a student who self-harms is told to stop but is not given alternate mechanisms for coping with their feelings, they will likely revert back to NSSI.

There are a variety of techniques and behaviors to help students manage their experiences. These are arranged according to categories of distress, although all of them can be helpful to students who are trying not to self-injure for any reason.

REPLACEMENT STRATEGIES

Reach Out to Others

- Phone a friend.
- Call 1-800-DONT-CUT.
- Go out and be around people.

Express Yourself

- Write down your feelings in a diary.
- Cry as a way to express your sadness or frustration.
- Draw or color.

Keep Busy

- Play a game.
- Listen to music.
- Read.
- Take a shower.
- Open a dictionary and learn new words.
- Do homework.
- Cook.
- Dig in the garden.
- Clean.
- Watch a feel-good movie.

Do Something Mindful

- Count down slowly from 10 to 0.
- Breathe slowly, in through the nose and out through the mouth.
- Focus on objects around you and thinking about how they look, sound, smell, taste, and feel.
- Do yoga.
- Meditate.
- Learn breathing exercises to aid relaxation.
- Concentrate on something that makes you happy: good friends, good times, laughter, etc.

Release Your Frustrations

- Throw ice cubes at a brick wall.
- Throw eggs in the shower.
- Rip apart an old magazine or phone book.
- Smash fruit with a bat or hammer.
- Throw darts.
- Punch pillows.
- Scream into a pillow.
- Slam doors.
- Yell or sing at the top of your lungs.
- Exercise.

Express Pain and Intense Emotions

- Paint, draw, or scribble on a big piece of paper with red ink or paint.
- Write in a journal to express your feelings.
- Compose a poem or song to say what you feel.
- Write down any negative feelings and then rip the paper up.
- Listen to music that expresses what you're feeling.

Feel Guilty or Deserve Punishment

- List as many good things about yourself as you can.
- Read something good that someone has written about you.
- Talk to someone who cares about you.
- Do something nice for someone else.
- Remember when you've done something good.
- Think about why you feel guilty and how you might be able to change it.

Feel Sad or Depressed

- Take a bath or hot shower.
- Pet or cuddle a dog or cat.
- Wrap yourself in a warm/weighted blanket.
- Massage your neck, hands, and feet.
- Listen to calming music.
- Do something slow and soothing.
- Give yourself a present.
- Hug a loved one.
- Make a list of things that make you happy.
- Do something nice for someone else.
- Smell sweet-smelling essential oils.
- Smooth lotion onto the parts of yourself you want to hurt.
- Call a friend.
- Watch TV or read.

Feel Numb or Disconnected

- Call a friend (you don't have to talk about self-harm).
- Take a cold shower or bath.
- Hold an ice cube in the crook of your arm or leg.
- Chew something with a very strong taste, like chili peppers, peppermint, ginger root, or a grapefruit peel.
- Go online to a self-help website, chat room, or message board.
- Squeeze ice.
- List the many uses for a random object. (For example, what are all the things you can do with a twist tie?)
- Put a finger into a frozen food (like ice cream).
- Slap a tabletop hard.
- Stomp your feet on the ground.
- Focus on how it feels to breathe. Notice the way your chest and stomach move with each breath.

Release Anger or Tension

- Exercise vigorously (run, dance, jump rope, or hit a punching bag).
- Punch a cushion or mattress or scream into your pillow.
- Squeeze a stress ball or squish Play-Doh or clay.
- Rip something up (sheets of paper, a magazine).
- Make some noise (play an instrument, bang on pots and pans).
- Slash an empty plastic soda bottle or a piece of heavy cardboard or an old shirt or sock.
- Squeeze ice.
- Do something that will give you a sharp sensation, like eating lemon.
- Make a soft cloth doll to represent the things you are angry at. Cut and tear it instead of yourself.
- Flatten aluminum cans for recycling, seeing how fast you can go.
- Pick up a stick and hit a tree.
- Use a pillow to hit a wall, pillow-fight style.
- On a sketch or photo of yourself, mark in red ink what you want to do. Cut and tear the picture.
- Make clay models and cut or smash them.
- Clean.
- Bang pots and pans.
- Stomp around in heavy shoes.
- Play handball or tennis.

Substitutes for the Cutting Sensation
• Use a red marker pen to draw on your skin where you might usually cut.
• Rub ice cubes over your skin where you might usually cut.
• Place rubber bands on your wrists, arms, or legs, and snap them instead of cutting.
• Putting stickers on the parts of your body you want to injure.
• Drawing slashing lines on paper.
• Paint on your skin with red watercolor or tempera paint.
• Drawing on the areas you want to cut using ice that you've made by dropping six or seven drops of red food color into each of the ice-cube tray wells.

A Student's Story

From the outside looking in, my life seemed fairly perfect. An only child, loving parents, pets, I lived near the beach, I had a lot of friends, my home life was good, and I made good grades. But on the inside I was lonely. I had a lot of anger. I resented my parents for my lack of love. My perception wasn't clear. I began to cut in middle school and stopped in high school. I experimented with other types of self-harm. I needed an outlet for my anger and hurt and loss. Thankfully, one day I decided that this wasn't helping my life. It was making me miserable. So I stopped. I was always able to stop; I just didn't know how to control my emotions. But thankfully I have learned. I poured my heart and soul into journaling. I had found a safe place to express my feelings. I wrote deep and dark poems. I could almost feel the anger seep out of me and become the ink in which I wrote. It was like magic. ~Blake

QUESTIONS to CONSIDER

1. How are students encouraged to express themselves at your school?

2. How do adults respond if a student expresses a negative emotion?

3. What support is needed for educators to be prepared to accept students' negative or distressful feelings without fear or judgement?

KEY POINTS

- If a student who self-harms is told to stop but is not given alternate mechanisms for coping with their feelings, they will likely turn back to NSSI.

- Replacement strategies can help the student express emotions without causing physical damage to the body.

5 How Can Teachers Help Students with NSSI?

Teachers can be a powerful advocate for students who engage in self-injury. It is important for all educators to learn about the causes, signs, and healthy interventions for NSSI, and review the school's protocol for supporting students who self-injure. Teachers are in a position to look for the warning signs listed in chapter 2. When they do identify a student who is self-injuring, teachers can play a key role in their well-being by expressing their concern and listening to these students without judgment.

Prevention Techniques

Although engaging in self-injury is solely the student's choice, teachers can implement prevention techniques in their classroom that may deter NSSI.

Reinforce positive stress management

Stress is a part of our daily lives. It can be the result of both positive and negative events. Learning how to manage stress in a healthy and productive manner can keep it from becoming *distress*. Distress is continued exposure to stressful situations that lead to overwhelming feelings and a sense of helplessness to do anything about our circumstances. Distress puts students at greater risk of using unhealthy coping strategies such as self-injury, alcohol or substance abuse, or other risky behavior.

A variety of experiences and circumstances can cause stress in students' lives. Both seemingly positive and negative experiences can result in stress.

Academic Stressors:

- Tests
- Homework
- Class presentations
- Answering questions in class
- Projects – both individual and group
- Accessing resources and materials for school
- Standardized tests
- Learning virtually
- Achieved goals
- Academic awards
- Managing learning difficulties
- Graduation/Promotion

Personal and Social Stressors:

- Changes in relationships
- Conflict with friends
- Romantic relationships
- Social media
- Fitting in
- Job interviews

- Work

- Financial concerns (both not having money and having money can be a stressor)

- Extracurricular activities

- Athletic opportunities

- Competitions

- Being recognized for outstanding work or achievement

- Transportation

Family or Environmental Stressors:

- Parent's divorce

- Change in guardianship

- Parent/guardian marriage

- Incarceration

- Family member's illness

- Increased responsibilities at home

- Caring for siblings

- Contributing to family income

- Death of a loved one

- Food insecurity

- Pregnancy

- Changes in one's living situation

Even in the best of circumstances, students can find themselves stressed and distressed. It is important for adults to recognize both positive and negative stressors and look for signs of stress in students, particularly those whose history would make them a higher risk factor for NSSI.

When you recognize a student showing symptoms of stress, coach them about positive approaches to dealing with their internal dynamics. Physical exercise, meditation, laughing with a friend, listening to music or any number of other outlets can provide the release the tension a student feels.

Teaching and Modeling Self-Care

Self-care is an effective stress management technique for both students and adults. Prioritizing and promoting activities that increase relaxation, rest, nutrition, exercise, fun, and healthy relationships minimizes the negative consequences of stress. Encourage students to practice self-care. Integrate self-care and wellness activities in academic content. Practice mindfulness in your class, particularly before tests or presentations. Model your own self-care practices for your students. This includes how we speak about our own responsibilities. When we wear our busyness like a badge of pride, we are equating productivity to self-worth, and we are sending our students the message that if they are not overwhelmed with lots of responsibilities, then they are somehow not important enough.

Creating Safe Learning Spaces

Teachers can also be safe outlets for students to talk about the stress they feel. Create a learning environment where all students feel valued and important. Make yourself available to your students. Let them see that you can listen without judgement and be an advocate for them. Practice community circles or morning meetings and discuss strategies for managing stress effectively. Get to know your students and watch for changes in behavior that may be a sign they are experiencing stress and distress. Reach out to your students when you observe these changes and offer support. Remind them of the strategies that you have taught them. Connect them to the school counselor if they need something more than redirection and encouragement. These strategies may not prevent every student from engaging in self-harm, but most students (and teachers) will be better off from them.

When You Think a Student Is Self-Injuring

School personnel are often the first adults to know that a student is engaging in NSSI. They may see the wounds or scars on the student, or another student may share their concern about a friend who is self-injuring. Sometimes, the student may disclose their self-harming behavior to a trusted teacher or counselor.

Recognizing the signs of NSSI is important, but how you respond to a student who is showing those signs is just as important. These students need a calm, supportive, and non-judgmental presence to walk with them through the difficulties.

Respond with Calm and Understanding

Both the language and tone the educator uses in their response can have a significant impact on whether the student accepts support. When interacting with a student who is (or is suspected of) self-injuring, always maintain a sympathetic attitude. Responding to the student in a calm and understanding manner should be the goal. The student may feel shame or embarrassment about their behavior. Harsh disciplinary actions for the self-injurious behavior can further shame the student and make them resistant to get assistance. Acknowledge and validate the feelings that trigger them to self-injure. Regardless of the individual, it is *critical* to demonstrate calmness, kindness, and acceptance when a student discloses their self-injury.

Take Action

If a student self-discloses NSSI behavior, it is important to be honest with the student about the school protocol requiring them to share their knowledge of self-injury with the designated person, often the school counselor. You (or the counselor) should assure the student that all information shared about the student's self-injury is strictly confidential.

If another student has shared concern about a classmate self-injuring or if the teacher has observed warning signs of NSSI, a conversation with the student is warranted. The teacher should ask simple questions to help determine whether the student has purposefully self-harmed. When students deny engaging in self-injury, the teacher should still share their concern with the school counselor. If the student acknowledges the self-harm, explain the school's protocol and assure the student that they will be supported.

If a teacher is not sure if the student is engaging in self-harm, they still should take action. However, they should never try to handle the situation on their own. Refer the student to the school counselor, social worker, or psychologist for further assessment, and follow-up to make sure communication has taken place. These mental health providers are trained to assess students to determine their level of engagement in NSSI as well as the risk for escalating behaviors such as suicidal ideation.

Prioritize Medical Needs

If a teacher observes that a wound is fresh, they should contact the school nurse to assess the severity of the injury and make sure the wound is properly treated. Teachers should not attempt to treat a wound or tissue damage. If the school nurse is not available, the teacher should contact the school's first responder team for assistance. Specific steps for assessing a student's medical needs should be included in the school's self-injury protocol.

A Student's Story

My home life was unpredictable. On the outside I acted like I could handle the arguments and fighting. The fighting was frequent, and my escape was to draw until I couldn't stand it any longer. Then a blade was my next solution. Self-harm wasn't a bad thing. It was my easy way out. But after so long, I quit trying to hide the scars. I no longer cared if others saw me struggle. They wouldn't understand anyway. When so many people saw only what they wanted to see, when so many people misjudged, mistreated and misunderstood me, I could never see the "light at the end of the tunnel." Over the years those around me saw it as attention seeking. They never understood. Why does society think that every home is the same? Why did people look at my body and judge me for what I had done? They had no idea what my home life was like. Why should they? They'd never stopped to ask what the marks were for, or why I had cut so deep. They never asked.~ Malik

QUESTIONS to CONSIDER

1. What strategies do you (and other teachers) use to check in with your students?

2. How can you incorporate stress management techniques within your classroom?

3. How can you let your students know that you see them and want to support them?

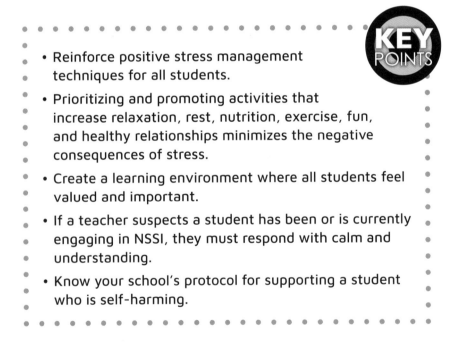

KEY POINTS

- Reinforce positive stress management techniques for all students.

- Prioritizing and promoting activities that increase relaxation, rest, nutrition, exercise, fun, and healthy relationships minimizes the negative consequences of stress.

- Create a learning environment where all students feel valued and important.

- If a teacher suspects a student has been or is currently engaging in NSSI, they must respond with calm and understanding.

- Know your school's protocol for supporting a student who is self-harming.

6

How Can School Counselors Help Students with NSSI?

School counselors can be important advocates for students who are engaging in self-injurious behaviors. They are responsible for delivering a school counseling program that includes both prevention and intervention strategies focused on the social and emotional development of all students. NSSI is rooted in emotional dysregulation, poor stress management, and high levels of anxiety. These are all areas that a school counselor can address through a variety of activities.

Prevention

School counselors have the opportunity to teach students emotional regulation skills through their school counseling curriculum. All students can benefit from learning how to identify a variety of feelings, the triggers that cause them, and how to manage them in an appropriate way. These strategies can be reinforced in small group and individual counseling.

There are numerous resources for teaching stress management skills. Most SEL programs include stress management. The Collaborative for Academic, Social, and Emotional Learning (CASEL) has a wealth of information on best practices for SEL interventions and a robust list of specific SEL programs. For elementary and middle school students, Trevor Romain and Elizabeth Verdick's

Stress Can Really Get on Your Nerves is a great resource for teaching students about identifying and managing stress. *Fighting Invisible Tigers* by Earl Hipp is another great resource for helping high school students cope with daily stressors and reduce risky behaviors such as self-injury.

https://www.mtu.edu/well-being/resources/stress-management/
Michigan Tech Center for Student Mental Health and Well-being

Training for Staff

A key component of self-injury prevention and intervention is education and training. When teachers know more about NSSI, they can be better advocates for their students who may be engaging in it. School counselors can facilitate these trainings with the other medical and mental health providers in the school, such as the school nurse, school social worker, or school psychologist. Topics to cover in self-injury training for teachers and staff includes the following:

- Definition of self-injury
- Why students engage in self-injury
- Methods of self-injury
- Difference between self-injury and suicidality
- Signs and symptoms
- Replacement behaviors
- School's self-injury protocol
- Strategies to support a student that self-injures in the classroom

All staff should know what to do if they suspect a student has engaged in self-harm. Remind school staff that the school has established a team to assist them so teachers know that they do not have to handle this on their own.

Assessment Team

When the school has been alerted that a student is engaging in self-injury, several assessments must be conducted to determine the appropriate plan to support them. The initial assessment should be made by the school nurse or member of the first responder team. Typically, this person should have training to assess a medical situation. The purpose of this assessment is to evaluate the student's wound and make sure it is treated appropriately. If the evaluation indicates that the student needs significant medical intervention, then emergency services should be called so the student can get proper care. The wound severity, implements used, location of the injury, and observed number of scars from previous wounds should be noted during the evaluation and discussed with the team during the self-injury risk assessment.

If the medical evaluation shows that no further medical intervention is needed, the student should then be assessed to determine the risk and severity of the self-harm and develop an appropriate intervention plan. It is important to note that this self-injury risk assessment does not replace a full medical or mental health assessment conducted by a medical provider. It is appropriate for the school counselor to lead the assessment team. Other team members may include the school nurse, school social worker, school psychologist, administrator, and teacher. The student should participate in the assessment if they are not in an emotional crisis. As a member of the team, the student is able to share their own perspectives about their experiences and what might be beneficial interventions. It is not necessary to have the parent present at this point. Parents are an important member of the team when it is time to discuss interventions to support the student.

The counselor should explain the purpose of the assessment and remind the team about expectations regarding confidentiality. There are formal assessments that have been tested for reliability and validity. The **Assessing NSSI Severity Assessment** and the **Brief Non-Suicidal Self-Injury Assessment Tool**, both developed by the Cornell Research Program on Self-Injury and Recovery (CRPSIR), are examples of these formal assessments. However, the team may choose to utilize a more informal process. In that case, the school counselor should ask clear and concise questions such as:

- Where on your body do you typically injure?

- What do you typically use to injure?

- What do you do to care for the wounds?

- Have you ever hurt yourself more severely than intended?

- Have your wounds ever become infected?

- Have you ever seen a doctor because you were worried about a wound?

Overall, questions should aim to assess the history, frequency, types of methods used, triggers, psychological purpose, disclosure, previous attempts to seek support, and past history and/or current presence of suicidal ideation. The student's answers to these questions will provide the team with important information to determine the student's risk for repeated self-injurious episodes, their capacity for self-care, the support the school can provide, and what community or medical resources should be considered.

One last consideration for the assessment team is a suicide risk assessment. We know that engaging in NSSI does not equate to suicidality, but self-injury can be a warning sign that suicide may become an option later, especially if the cause of the distress is not effectively addressed. Conducting the suicide assessments provides additional information for the team to consider when developing an intervention plan for the student. There are several suicide risk assessment tools that school counselors, school social workers, school psychologists, and school nurses may be familiar with. The National Institute of Mental Health has developed the **ASQ: Ask Suicide Screening Questions**. In addition, **Question, Persuade, Refer (QPR)** is widely used in schools to conduct suicide risk assessments. **ASIST (Applied Suicide Intervention Skills Training)** is another option if anyone on the team has been trained in that assessment. If the team determines that the student is at risk for suicidal ideation, proceed with the school's suicide intervention protocol.

The Cornell Research Program on Self-Injury and Recovery (CRPSIR) has established a scale to determine the student's level of risk severity.

Characteristics of high severity class:

✓ Greater than 11 lifetime incidents of NSSI

✓ Use more than two methods (often more than three methods)

✓ Use at least one method likely to cause severe tissue damage, such as cutting or carving the body, burning areas of the body, breaking bones, dripping acid onto skin, and ingesting a caustic substance(s) or sharp object(s)

✓ About 43 percent of those who reported NSSI fell into the high severity class. Of those in this class, about 70 percent were female.

✓ This class is more likely than to report suicidality, disordered eating, struggling with other mental health challenges/disorders, and history of sexual, emotional and/or physical trauma than peers not engaging in NSSI. They are also more likely to have been in therapy or to need therapy.

✓ Compared to the other NSSI severity groups, they are more likely to have friends who self-injure, to show strong tendencies for NSSI addiction, and to have hurt themselves more severely than intended.

Characteristics of moderate severity class:

✓ Two to 10 lifetime incidents of NSSI

✓ Use two to three methods of self-injury

✓ Use at least one method likely to cause bruising or light tissue damage such as punching or banging oneself or other objects, sticking sharp objects into the skin (not including tattooing, body piercing, or needles used for medication use), and self-bruising.

✓ Almost 40 percent of those who report NSSI fell into this moderate group, and 60% of this group were men.

✓ More likely to report suicidality, disordered eating, emotional abuse, and a history of therapy than peers not engaging in NSSI

Characteristics of low severity class:

✓ Majority report fewer than 10 lifetime incidents of NSSI

✓ Vast majority use only one method of self-injury

- ✓ All methods likely to cause superficial tissue damage such as scratching or pinching until bleeding occurs or marks remain on the skin; intentionally preventing wounds from healing

- ✓ 15% of those reporting NSSI fell into this category; 72% of this group were female.

- ✓ More likely to report suicidality, disordered eating, emotional abuse, and history of therapy than peers not engaging in NSSI.

From the Cornell Research Program on Self-Injury and Recovery
http://www.selfinjury.bctr.cornell.edu/perch/resources/cprsitseverityassessment.pdf

Intervention Plan

An intervention plan is the written documentation of specific actions the team will take to support the student. It should be developed collaboratively with the students, parents, and school staff. Generally, medical or community providers are not included in the intervention plan; however, the students and/or parents could pursue those outside supports. The intervention plan should include reasonable goals and a date to review the plan and make revisions as needed. Specific interventions for teachers, administrators, and parents are discussed in their respective chapters. The following interventions are primarily for the school counselor, school social worker, or school psychologist.

Low-Risk Students

Students with little history of self-injury, a manageable amount of external stress, some appropriate coping skills, and some external support will require less complex intervention plans. It is important to work with the student to come up with strategies for handling stress and for checking in with a trusted adult at school when they begin to feel like they may be at risk for self-injury or other unhealthy behaviors. Monitoring student behavior through observation, teacher reports, and periodic check-ins is also warranted for a brief time following a self-injury event.

Higher-Risk Students

Students who report frequent self-injury practices, who use high lethality methods, and who are experiencing chronic internal and external stress with few positive supports or coping skills will likely require a more extensive intervention plan. It is important to note that students should be engaged as active participants in the development of the plan, even in cases where they show resistance. In these cases, the school counselor participates in the intervention plan in multiple ways: helping the family identify medical or mental health providers; providing individual supports when the student is in school; and managing the intervention plan.

Identifying Medical or Mental Health Providers

Share a list of local providers who specialize in self-injury and/or adolescent behavior. In addition to those local providers, there are additional resources to help identify an appropriate specialist.

- *S.A.F.E. Alternatives.* This website provides a listing of therapists in the area who are trained in self-injury treatment. (https://selfinjury.com/referrals/therapists)

- American Psychological Association. This organization can provide a list of therapists based on location, specialty, and age group. (https://locator.apa.org/)

- Insurance company. Parents may also consider contacting their insurance company for a list of providers covered under their policy.

Individual Support

The school counselor is equipped to support the student through individual counseling, focusing on self-awareness and stress management techniques. If there are underlying issues contributing to the increased distress, such as relationship issues, academic struggles, or communication challenges, the counselor can assist with solution-focused or cognitive behavioral counseling. Examples of these interventions include:

Stress Management. Replacement strategies are behaviors and actions that students can utilize instead of the self-injurious action they have previously used when they feel stressed. These coping mechanisms encourage the student to respond differently when they feel like cutting or hurting themselves. Replacement strategies can help the student to express emotions without causing physical damage to the body. Chapter 5 includes a variety of replacement behaviors that can be used for various situations.

The school counselor can work with the student to identify several replacement behaviors they can use while at school. It is important that the student's teachers are aware of the replacement behaviors the student may engage in while in their classroom. The school counselor should help facilitate conversations between the student and teacher(s) to address any concerns and make sure that the student is not disciplined for using the replacement behaviors.

Self-Awareness. Helping the student become more aware of their own strengths and skills can help them feel more empowered to deal with their stressors. Encourage them to engage in activities that build a sense of achievement. In addition, challenging the student to do one positive thing every day can lead to a sense of achievement and contentment. Remind the student to pay more attention to the positive events in their lives. Things that bring joy have been shown to decrease negative moods and increase positive moods.

Cognitive Behavioral Counseling. Changing your thoughts is easier than changing your feelings. Thoughts play a critical role in how we experience a situation. Help the student notice when they first become upset and recognize the thoughts that are causing that difficult emotion. Questions the student can ask themselves:

- What is it that's *really* pushing my buttons here?

- Why am I reacting so strongly?

- What's the worst (or best) that could happen?

- How important will this be tomorrow? Next week? Next month?

Making Referrals. NSSI does not always manifest as part of another mental health disorder. The student may need academic accommodations in the classroom if the self-injury is interfering with their ability to learn. If a student does have medical diagnosis, then a special education or Section 504 evaluation should be considered.

School social workers may be able to provide more intensive counseling services for students. They can also assist families in access medical or community resources to address the students' behavior.

The school counselor can be a strong support when the student is ready to stop hiding the scars of their self-injuring. For a student who is still engaging in self-harm, revealing the scars may actually trigger additional NSSI episodes. However, when a student has progressed in their recovery, no longer hiding the evidence of their prior self-injury can be a positive step. The school counselor can help the student prepare for this important step by:

- Acknowledging that this is the student's choice and that this may be a positive step for them.

- Discussing with the student how they will handle possible intrusive questions and negative comments

- Developing a clear plan for how the student can alert the appropriate school personnel should any bullying occur. Ensure that the specified person is aware of the plan.

- Scheduling regular check-ins with the student to monitor the situation and provide ongoing support

Case Management

The school counselor will often serve as the leader for the assessment team. Because of their training, they are in a position to conduct an initial assessment, engage the parents to partner with the school to support the student, provide some interventions, and monitor the intervention plan. Multiple counselors in a school may fulfill these responsibilities for their own student caseloads. Although most students do not engage in multiple self-injurious episodes, treatment for the underlying issues may take some time. The school counselor can ensure that the student continues to receive support throughout the entire process.

A Student's Story

I self-harmed for years by burning my skin. I felt so alone. One of my close friends told me that talking to our counselor would help relieve some of the feelings I had been feeling. It was like this huge burden was lifted when I told someone I trusted about my self-harm. I got the help I needed. Because of the support I have received, I haven't harmed myself or thought about harming myself in two years! If you feel like hurting yourself, get help and stop letting bad coping skills hinder your life. ~August

QUESTIONS to CONSIDER

1. What programs or activities are included in your school's counseling program to help students learn to regulate their emotions with healthy coping skills?

2. What processes are in place to foster collaboration between the school counselor and other mental health educators, such as the school social worker and school psychologist?

3. What additional training or information should the school counselor receive to prepare for supporting students who engage in self-injury?

KEY POINTS

- All students can benefit from learning how to identify a variety of feelings, the triggers that cause them, and how to manage them in an appropriate way.

- School counselors can assist with education and training for school staff, a key component of self-injury prevention and intervention.

- The assessment team, including the school counselor, school nurse, and administrator, will determine the level of risk of the student injuring themselves again.

- An intervention plan should be developed based on the outcome of the initial risk assessment.

How Can 7 Administrators Help Students with NSSI?

Administrators are responsible for all aspects of the school community. They are the academic leaders, school climate managers, behavior supervisors, and personnel directors. These functions can have a positive impact on students engaging in NSSI. Administrators set the tone for establishing expectations as well as how those expectations are met. Unstable, unpredictable, or invalidating environments contribute to adolescent anxiety and frustration, which are some of the overwhelming feelings at the root of self-injurious behaviors. The antidote for that anxiety and frustration is structure and empathy. Administrators lead the efforts that contribute to building that environment, especially for students who engage in NSSI.

A positive school climate supports the academic achievement and the mental health of all students. The foundation of a supportive learning environment includes clear expectations for students and adults, a shared definition of success, attention to the social and emotional development of students and adults, a connection of learning goals to students' future, support for students' exhibiting a variety of needs, and engagement of the school community, including parents. We will examine how to build this foundation specifically for students who engage in NSSI. Additional strategies for developing a strong learning environment for students experiencing anxiety and stress can be found in my first book in this series, *Anxiety: Worry, Stress, and Fear*. Strategies for ensuring your school climate is trauma-informed and supportive of students with adverse childhood experiences can be found in Dr. Melissa Reeves' book, *Trauma and Adverse Childhood Experiences*.

School Protocol for Students Who Self-Injure

A school protocol for students who self-injure identifies specific actions that should occur when: 1) a student discloses self-harm, 2) a student engages in self-injury at school, or 3) a student is suspected of using NSSI. The protocol also documents the school's procedures for consistently addressing these students' needs. The protocol should be developed by a school leadership team that includes both a medical and mental health professional, typically the school nurse and school counselor, respectively. If a school has a first responder team trained to address medical situations, employing this team to create a self-injury protocol is appropriate. Once developed, the entire school faculty and staff should review and commit to following the guidelines set in the protocol. Several key issues should be included in the self-injury protocol.

Referral. When an adult in the school becomes aware that a student has recently engaged or is currently engaging in NSSI, whom do they need to contact? If there is an immediate medical need, contacting the school nurse or a member of the first responder team would be appropriate. If schools have protocols for medical emergencies, that plan may be sufficient for students with fresh wounds. If the student does not have a physical injury that requires immediate attention, the student should be referred directly to the school counselor. Protocol should include contingencies for a second contact person if the original contact person is unavailable. Plans for covering a teacher's class so they can accompany the student to the contact person should also be addressed.

Medical Evaluation. Schools may have a plan in place to address medical emergencies. These plans should be appropriate for a student who has an immediate medical need. If a student's injuries are severe or life-threatening, or if the student is expressing suicidality, emergency services should be contacted. Parents or guardians should also be notified at this point. If the student's injuries can be effectively treated by the school nurse or first responder, then they should be referred directly to the school counselor once the injury has been addressed.

Risk Assessment. A student who is engaging in NSSI needs to be assessed for the level of risk they pose to themselves. It is important to determine if the student is expressing any suicidal ideation along with the self-injurious behavior. The school's protocol should establish policies to guide the initial risk assessment, such as: if the assessment will be conducted by a team or a singular individual; whether the student will be a contributing member of the assessment team; and how to engage the parents or guardians in the assessment. Specific assessment instruments or processes should also be included in the protocol. A school counselor, school social worker, or school psychologist should be trained to conduct these assessments. An example of an assessment process is included in this chapter.

Parent Engagement. The self-injury protocol should include a policy regarding parental notification and contact. In most cases, parents/guardians can be a helpful resource for supporting the student who is using self-injury by sharing information about the student's home environment. Parents can ensure that the student will receive care by initiating outpatient counseling for the child and/or family, agreeing to having the student receive enhanced academic and/or counseling supports within the school itself, and providing releases of information to the school so that the team may communicate with any outside professionals assisting the student. Engaging parents provides them with an opportunity to ask questions, share parental concerns, and dispel any myths about self-injury that the parents might have. Since state and local laws surrounding student confidentiality and parent disclosure may vary, the procedures for contacting parents in this situation should align to district policies, and maintain the best interest of the child.

Intervention. This section of the protocol should define what needs to happen to support the student, as well as who is responsible for monitoring each of those interventions. Once a risk assessment has been completed, the team can make recommendations regarding next steps for the student. NSSI is not something that should be treated only within the school environment. School supports as well as community resources should be included in the intervention plan. In most cases, a student who engages in self-injury will benefit from working with a counselor or therapist outside of school to identify the sources of distress and engage in treatment to address them. Identifying specialists or organizations that specialize in NSSI for families can expedite getting the student assistance. Schools can implement strategies to support the student while they are at school. Working with the school counselor to practice stress management techniques, allowing the student to use appropriate replacement strategies in the classroom, and adjusting the student's academic workload are examples of interventions that can be put into place for the student. The intervention plan may also include specific goals the student will work toward.

Follow-Up. A plan for when and how to check in with the student communicates the school's commitment to support them. The protocol should include expectations for following up on the implementation plan for the student. Methods for gather feedback from each area of support should also be identified.

Sample Protocol

The Cornell Research Program on Self-Injury and Recovery provides an example of a self-injury protocol for schools.

SCHOOL PROTOCOL PROCESS

The flowchart below can help school staff decide what action(s) to take after discovering that a student may be engaging in self-injury.

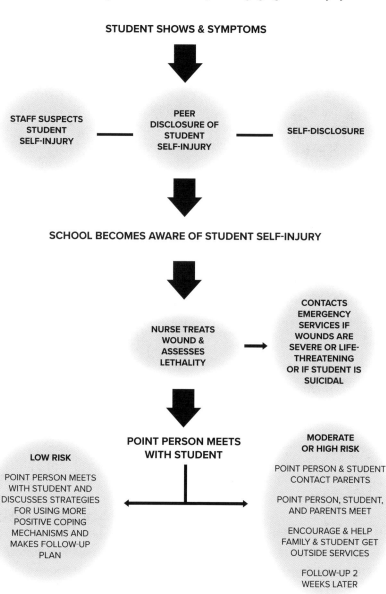

STUDENT SHOWS & SYMPTOMS

STAFF SUSPECTS STUDENT SELF-INJURY — **PEER DISCLOSURE OF STUDENT SELF-INJURY** — **SELF-DISCLOSURE**

SCHOOL BECOMES AWARE OF STUDENT SELF-INJURY

NURSE TREATS WOUND & ASSESSES LETHALITY → **CONTACTS EMERGENCY SERVICES IF WOUNDS ARE SEVERE OR LIFE-THREATENING OR IF STUDENT IS SUICIDAL**

POINT PERSON MEETS WITH STUDENT

LOW RISK

POINT PERSON MEETS WITH STUDENT AND DISCUSSES STRATEGIES FOR USING MORE POSITIVE COPING MECHANISMS AND MAKES FOLLOW-UP PLAN

MODERATE OR HIGH RISK

POINT PERSON & STUDENT CONTACT PARENTS

POINT PERSON, STUDENT, AND PARENTS MEET

ENCOURAGE & HELP FAMILY & STUDENT GET OUTSIDE SERVICES

FOLLOW-UP 2 WEEKS LATER

From the Cornell Research Program on Self-Injury and Recovery

Training and Education

Administrators can ensure that all faculty and staff receive training on NSSI and the school's protocol for supporting students who self-injure. The training should include a definition, signs and symptoms, myths, the difference between NSSI and suicidality, replacement strategies, contagion, supporting a student who is self-injuring, and how to engage parents. The training can be delivered by the team that developed the protocol or through various community organizations. A wealth of resources for schools can be found at the Cornell University Self-injury & Recovery Resources (http://www.selfinjury.bctr.cornell.edu/index.html). It may also be necessary to conduct refresher trainings throughout the school year, particularly if the school community experiences a stress-inducing event such as a pandemic or student death.

Staff Resources

Administrators are positioned to identify the appropriate staff and personnel to address NSSI effectively and efficiently. Because of the varied nature of NSSI, it is important to have a team of educators who can provide support to a student engaging in self-injurious behaviors. Once the team has been selected, the administrator determines the role of each member on the team. An example of assigned roles includes:

School Nurse

- Give direct care to any wounds
- Evaluate for further medical concerns
- Contact emergency services if the student has significant or life-threatening injuries
- Ensure that the school counselor follows up with the student
- Facilitate training for faculty and staff

School Counselor

- Serve as the coordinator for the assessment team

- Consult with referring teacher
- Contact parents/guardian
- Work with student on appropriate coping techniques/ replacement strategies
- Initiate follow-up of assessment team to review implementation plan
- Facilitate training for faculty and staff

School Social Worker

- Participate on the assessment team
- Support parents in finding appropriate community resources
- Provide individual counseling
- Communicate with parents/guardians
- Review progress of implementation plan
- Facilitate training for faculty and staff

School Psychologist

- Participate on the assessment team
- Provide individual counseling
- Address academic impact of self-injury
- Review progress of implementation plan
- Facilitate training for faculty and staff

A Student's Story

I knew from an early age I didn't fit in. My parents were always proud of their little girl, but the problem was that I didn't feel like a girl. I felt trapped in a body not meant for me. I felt like something was wrong with me. Because my body was not "right," I started carving into it. It was all I could do to punish my physical self for betraying my inner self. I kept the scars on my stomach hidden until I could no longer pretend. I found an online group for students like me. Once I understood what it meant to be trans, I was able to find the words to tell my parents. I was a boy and needed to be treated as one. It was hard initially but we went to a therapist and are working through it. I learned that I don't deserve to be punished for being who I am. ~Brando

QUESTIONS to CONSIDER

1. How does your school's climate support students' mental health?

2. What school staff members have training and expertise to develop a self-injury protocol that supports positive student interventions?

3. What other policies or procedures might be helpful in creating a self-injury protocol?

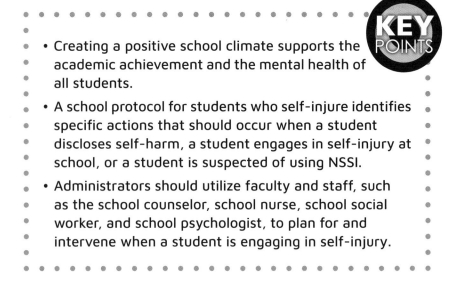

KEY POINTS

- Creating a positive school climate supports the academic achievement and the mental health of all students.

- A school protocol for students who self-injure identifies specific actions that should occur when a student discloses self-harm, a student engages in self-injury at school, or a student is suspected of using NSSI.

- Administrators should utilize faculty and staff, such as the school counselor, school nurse, school social worker, and school psychologist, to plan for and intervene when a student is engaging in self-injury.

8

What is Social Contagion?

Self-injurious behaviors often carry with them an interesting phenomenon called social contagion. Social contagion is a type of social influence. Social contagion theory states that ideas or behaviors, much like an illness or disease, can spread through populations unintentionally. Individuals can learn about or adopt a new attitude or behavior from the people with whom the interact.

Social contagion with NSSI refers to the increased likelihood that multiple members of a social group will engage in self-injury if they become aware that another member is self-harming. Self-injurious behaviors are particularly susceptible to social contagion because of their provocative nature and powerful ability to communicate. When students are struggling emotionally or socially, witness another peer engage in these risky behaviors, and perceive that they are getting attention or support, these "witnesses" may consider imitating the risky behavior with the hopes of either reducing their own pain or getting the attention they witness their peer receiving. The risk for contagion is increased when popular students are engaged in self-injury or when self-injury is used as a means for students to feel a sense of cohesiveness or belonging to a particular group.

Social contagion is not limited to physical proximity. In fact, media and social media have had a significant impact on increases of self-harm and suicidal behaviors, particular in adolescent populations.

When characters in television shows or movies participate in self-injury to deal with a challenging situation, it legitimizes those behaviors and communicates to those watching that this might be an acceptable coping strategy. If the student observes characters using self-injury across different shows, they will likely develop an increased tolerance to the dangerous behaviors. Many students engaging in NSSI report feeling more comfortable in online communities rather than in-person groups. In some of these communities, self-injuring is a normalized behavior so a student may no longer feel different or alone. They may also learn additional methods of self-injury as well as ways of hiding it from the adults in their lives.

Adolescents consume a wealth of information from social media and media. They learn what is expected of them by what they see on Instagram, Snapchat, and TikTok. They communicate in abbreviations and emojis on these platforms, which do not allow for meaningful conversations. Students seek out information through media, especially if they do not feel comfortable asking an adult for assistance. Students have access to a spectrum of ideas and behaviors, as well as a multitude of "truths" stemming from perspectives as varied as people on the planet. So, in addition to seeing NSSI more frequently, media intake (and social media in particular) can increase the emotional and social stress a student experiences, which raises their risk for self-injurious behaviors if they do not have appropriate coping mechanisms.

As soon as "grown-ups" think they have created safeguards to protect students, tech savvy young people have navigated around those boundaries. Although educators have limited capacity to manage students' activity online, they can give students tools to help them navigate media more effectively. By teaching students to be critical consumers of information available in the media, they can learn to evaluate sources of information for credibility. The book, *Common Sense Education,* provides helpful resources for educators and schools to teach students digital literacy. It is also important to remind students of other supports and resources available to them "in real life." These prevention activities will not eliminate the possibility of social contagion related to self-injury, but it can reduce its influence on some students.

School Prevent of Social Contagion Associated with NSSI

The best intervention is prevention. When students know how to regulate their emotions and have appropriate coping strategies, they are less likely to engage in risky behaviors to manage their feelings. Promote a positive and safe learning environment for all students. Ensure school counselors include stress management techniques and self-awareness skills in the delivery of the school counseling program. Educate school faculty and staff on warning signs of anxiety, emotional dysregulation, self-injury, and suicidal ideation. Develop policies and protocols for supporting struggling students. Strategies for these prevention activities have been discussed earlier.

Even with the best prevention work, schools will likely experience a crisis, which could include a student engaging in self-injury. It is common for the recovery protocol from the crisis to include a plan to address the situation with students and the school community. However, a well-meaning plan to address NSSI in schools may unintentionally increase the chance of developing social contagion. Because social contagion is facilitated by communication, it is important to reduce communication about self-injury.

Schools can employ the following strategies to reduce the likelihood of additional students imitating self-injurious behaviors:

Discourage student disclosure. School officials are bound by law to protect a student's privacy through FERPA and HIPPA. However, a student can decide what information they want to share with others. It is important to advise the student engaging in self-injury not to share detailed information about their behaviors, show pictures or scars, or tell stories of episodes of self-injury with other students. Give them strategies of what to say if other students begin asking about what is going on. Statements such as "I'm okay," "I don't really want to talk about it," "Thanks for your concern," and please respect my privacy" can serve as deterrents from curious students. Remind the student of adults that they can talk to about their feelings so they know they have support at school.

Manage physical wounds. School staff should help self-injuring students to manage their scars and wounds. Visible scars, wounds, and cuts should be discouraged.

Avoid large assemblies. Large group assemblies, daily announcements, newsletters, or school social media platforms should not be used to address an episode or outbreak of NSSI.

Put NSSI into context. When educating youth about NSSI, discuss the behavior in the broader context of unhealthy coping strategies to stress and anxiety, including substance abuse or risk-taking activities. Educate students about signs of distress and how to use appropriate coping skills. Remind students about the supports available to them.

Address NSSI individually. When schools experience multiple students engaging in self-injury, each student should be treated individually. Group sessions with students who self-injure are not an effective intervention.

A Student's Story

I turned to cutting my sophomore year of high school when a friend of my who self-harmed glorified it. I came from a family of dysfunction. My parents were divorced when I was the age of 1 and both remarried few years later. I was forced to move with my mom and stepdad more than 10 hours from my dad and family at the age of 7. At a young age I felt like I had nobody to talk to, I didn't get along with my stepdad, and my mom and I didn't have the best relationship either. As I grew up, I didn't know how to express problems or feelings, I just let them be and go on with life. My sophomore year I began being bullied by my so-called friends. I felt betrayed, useless, and alone. My best friend at the time told me about how she cut and how the feeling of cutting your skin so deep took away the pain. I tried it not knowing that it would end up becoming an addiction and my inner demon. I would cut every time I began feeling stressed, mad, sad, alone—pretty much any way other than happy. As years kept going my urge to cut became stronger. I became suicidal and would even write out my letters to family. I would lie about self-harming, I would cut in places that people couldn't see, I would wear long sleeves in the middle of Summer. Nobody knew my secret. ~ Zahara

QUESTIONS to CONSIDER

1. What protocols are in place at your school to protect communications regarding student issues between faculty? Students?

2. What strategies can be utilized to support the student engaging in self-harm without bringing attention to the behavior?

3. How do school behavior expectations reinforce the use of positive coping strategies?

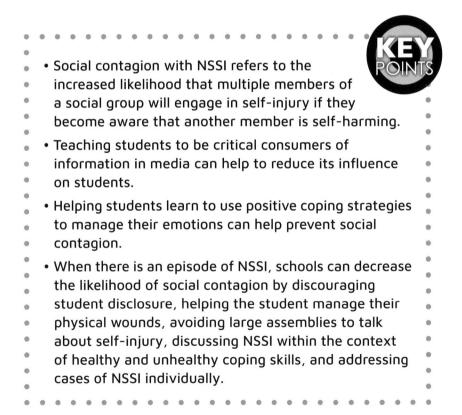

KEY POINTS

• Social contagion with NSSI refers to the increased likelihood that multiple members of a social group will engage in self-injury if they become aware that another member is self-harming.

• Teaching students to be critical consumers of information in media can help to reduce its influence on students.

• Helping students learn to use positive coping strategies to manage their emotions can help prevent social contagion.

• When there is an episode of NSSI, schools can decrease the likelihood of social contagion by discouraging student disclosure, helping the student manage their physical wounds, avoiding large assemblies to talk about self-injury, discussing NSSI within the context of healthy and unhealthy coping skills, and addressing cases of NSSI individually.

How Can Schools Partner with Parents to Help Students Who Self-Harm?

9

NSSI should not be treated solely within the school environment. When a student is engaging in self-injury, it is critical to engage the parents or guardians. They will need to initiate outside support for the student with medical and/or mental health providers. To facilitate getting that important assistance, school staff should approach the parents as partners with the shared goal of supporting the student. Considerations should be given to how the parents or guardians will be notified, potential parent reactions to the news that their child is self-injuring, specific action steps for parents, and resources that the school can provide to the student and parents. It is important to note that in cases when parents may not agree to further medical or mental health treatment, the school can take actions to support the student.

Parent Notification

It is the legal responsibility of the school to notify parents of their child's self-injury, even if the assessment team has determined that the student is not an immediate threat to themselves. Plans for parent notifications should be included in the school protocol and should be documented once notification has been made.

Once a student has disclosed NSSI to a school staff person and an assessment has been completed to ensure that they do not need immediate medical care, the student should be encouraged to call their parents themselves. They should do this with a trusted adult present, such as the school counselor or teacher. The school staff person should be prepared to discuss with the parent the school's protocol for supporting students that self-injure and ask the parent to come to the school to discuss the situation as soon as possible.

Some students may not feel like they can make that call themselves. They may fear their parents' reactions, or the triggering circumstances for self-injury may stem from parental or environmental conflict. In that case, it is advisable that the school counselor (or member of the assessment team) contact the parents, explain what has happened with their child, and invite them to come to the school to discuss the situation.

Reactions of Parents

School staff should expect to see a variety of reactions from parents when they learn that their child is injuring themselves. They will likely experience many emotions, such as shock, fear, confusion, and even frustration. Many worry that the self-injury means that their child wants to commit suicide. Some parents may feel guilty and start to question their own behaviors or feel bad because they did not see their child was hurting. If the parent seems to be struggling with guilt, it may be helpful to acknowledge their feelings and remind them that they can also get counseling for themselves during this difficult time. Other parents may not understand why someone would intentionally hurt themselves and deny that a problem exists. The school's role is to encourage the parents to try and understand what their child might be going through, recognize that their child is suffering, and approach their child from a nonjudgmental stance.

Some parents will respond immediately and come to the school ready to get their child help. Others may need a little more time to process their own feelings and thoughts about the situation.

The school's responsibility is to inform the parents about their child's self-injurious behavior and to encourage parents to seek counseling or treatment for the child. The school may need to educate parents on NSSI, clarify any myths or misconceptions about self-injury, and identify community resources available to support them all through this situation. Communicating about the resources within the school may encourage more collaboration with parents.

If the parents or guardians refuse to acknowledge their child's distress at all, the assessment team should discuss whether to contact the department of children's services about possible medical neglect. In some cases, parents may come to school and listen to the team but decide not to pursue any additional treatment or support for their child. In that case, it is helpful for the school to have the parent sign a statement that they are choosing to forego any medical or mental health treatment. This statement documents the school's attempt to meet its legal notification requirement. The student will still have access to the supports within the school, such as the school counselor, school social worker, or school psychologist.

Next Steps for Parents

Once parents have been notified that their child has engaged in NSSI and come to the school to discuss the situation, they will look to the school for what to do next. Setting up an intervention plan with steps outlined for the school, student, and parents can be helpful for everyone. Suggestions for the parent's next steps may include:

1. Attend to any physical wounds on their child.

2. Agree to several replacement strategies that their child can utilize as an alternate to self-injury.

3. Arrange for counseling for their child. The therapist may suggest family counseling in addition to individual counseling.

4. Consent to having their child receive enhanced academic and/or counseling supports at school as appropriate.

5. Provide releases of information to the school so that the school counselor may communicate with any outside professionals who are assisting the student.

6. Schedule a follow-up meeting with the assessment team within 2-4 weeks to review the intervention plan and make revisions if necessary.

Treatment for NSSI can be challenging and may take some time. Many parents spend a lot of their time and energy seeking help for their child; however, they ignore they own stress and anxiety. It is important to remind parents that they also need to establish their own supports. In addition to their own health and wellness, it is also an opportunity for them to model appropriate coping strategies for their child. There may even be stress management techniques that the family can utilize together.

Resources for Parents

Offering a list resources to parents can help them navigate what can be an overwhelming responsibility of getting their child assistance. Remember that when parents first become aware that their child has engaged in self-injury, they are often flooded with thoughts and feelings. Providing written copies of information can be helpful to parents when they reflect on the situation.

Examples of resources to share with parents include:

• Fact sheets about NSSI

- Replacement behaviors to suggest

- List of community resources specifically for NSSI

- Online resources

- Copy of Intervention Plan

- Copies of Release of Information

- Contact information for school counselor (or school social worker, school psychologist, lead contact person)

Many of these resources are available as downloadable resources with this book. Instructions for accessing these resources is included at the end of the book.

A Student's Story

Self-harm is something we can control. It is a war that I still am fighting. I used to believe that I was alone. It's as if I were inside this black hole and I just kept falling deeper and deeper. I realized that there are people who care and want the best for me. I realized it hurts them to see me like that. I learned that I am not alone. No one is. No matter how cold and horrible this world might seem, there will always be that spark of sunshine. I am learning that things do get better and the urges do stop. But we are the ones in control, we decide. I haven't fully recovered but I am trying. There are people around you that understand and want to help.
~Terrence

1. Does a school staff member have a collaborative relationship with the parents of a student who is self-injuring?

2. What supports are available for the parents of a student engaging in self-harm?

3. How can the team create a safe and calm environment for both the student and parents, especially during an initial meeting to discuss concerns about self-injury?

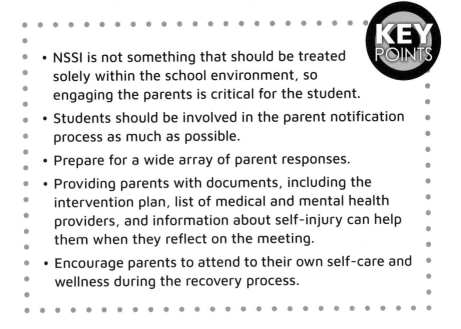

KEY POINTS

- NSSI is not something that should be treated solely within the school environment, so engaging the parents is critical for the student.
- Students should be involved in the parent notification process as much as possible.
- Prepare for a wide array of parent responses.
- Providing parents with documents, including the intervention plan, list of medical and mental health providers, and information about self-injury can help them when they reflect on the meeting.
- Encourage parents to attend to their own self-care and wellness during the recovery process.

10

Where Can I Find Out More About NSSI?

Organizations

Cornell Research Program on Self-Injury and Recovery (CRPSIR) seeks to understand, detect, treat, and prevent self-injury. Their work is intended to generate new research and insight into self-injury. They also aim to translate the growing body of knowledge about self-injury into resources and tools for those seeking to better understand, treat, and prevent it. http://www.selfinjury.bctr. cornell.edu/index.html

Self-injury Outreach and Support (SiOS) is a non-profit outreach initiative providing information and resources about self-injury to those who self-injure, those who have recovered, and those who want to help. http://sioutreach.org

To Write Love on Her Arms is a non-profit movement dedicated to presenting hope and finding help for people struggling with depression, addiction, self-injury, and suicide. TWLOHA exists to encourage, inform, inspire, and also to invest directly into treatment and recovery. https://twloha.com/

HelpGuide is a small independent nonprofit that runs one of the world's top 10 mental health websites. https://www.helpguide.org/articles/anxiety/cutting-and-self-harm.htm

Online Resources

Crisis Text Line
Text HOME to 741741 to reach a crisis counselor. Crisis Text Line serves anyone, in any type of crisis, providing access to free, 24/7 support via a medium people already use and trust: texting.

Your Life Your Voice: 99 Coping Skills provides an interactive list and print-out of 99 healthy coping skills and strategies. https://www.yourlifeyourvoice.org/pages/tip-99-coping-skills.aspx

Calm Harm is an award-winning app developed for teenage mental health using the basic principles of Dialectical Behavioral Therapy (DBT). Calm Harm provides tasks to help you resist or manage the urge to self-harm. https://calmharm.co.uk/#row1

Common Sense Education supports K–12 schools with an award-winning free Digital Citizenship Curriculum that prepares students with lifelong habits and skills, supports teachers with training and recognition, and engages families and communities with helpful tips and tools. https://www.commonsense.org/education/

Literature

See My Pain by Susan Bowman & Kaye Randall
This book provides a collection of strategies and activities to help children and adolescents who deliberately self-injure. A variety of hands-on creative arts approaches are featured that can be used in private practice and school settings.

Why Do I Hurt Myself? by Susan Bowman
Researchers have noted that students as young as 3rd grade are engaging in self-injurious behaviors. Through the story of Elisa, a 6th grade student that has begun engaging in self-injury, elementary students can learn healthy ways to deal with uncomfortable feelings and thoughts.

Research

International Consortium on Self-Injury in Educational Settings (ICSES) is an interdisciplinary and international research group consistent of leading researchers in the field of NSSI. Our research expertise covers psycho-social-cognitive factors, which underlie NSSI, neurobiology of NSSI, factors associated with stigma and the experience of recovery, the communications of NSSI online, education and training needs of school personnel, implementation and evaluation of school-based intervention, and the relationship between family functioning and NSSI. http://icsesgroup.org/about-us.

Brown, R. C., & Plener, P. L. "Non-suicidal self-injury in adolescence." *Current Psychiatry* Reports 19, no. 3 (2017): 20.

Dorko, L. A. "Literature review of the doctoral project development of a website for educators addressing how to understand, recognize, and respond to student self-injury." A doctoral project submitted to the faculty of the Graduate School of Psychology. https://educatorsandselfinjury.com/literature-review/

Gratz, K. L., Dixon-Gordon, K. L., Chapman, A. L., & Tull, M. T. "Diagnosis and characterization of DSM-5 nonsuicidal self-injury disorder using the clinician-administered nonsuicidal self-injury disorder index." *Assessment* 22, no. 5 (2015): 527-539.

Halicka, B. J., & Kiejna, A, A. (2018). "Non-suicidal self-injury (NSSI) and suicide: Criteria differentiation." *Advances in Clinical and Experimental Medicine* 27, no. 2 (2018).

Wester, K. L., Wachter Morris, C., & Williams, B. "Nonsuicidal self-injury in the schools: A tiered prevention approach for reducing social contagion." *Professional School Counseling* 21, no. 1 (2017): 1096-2409.

RESOURCES

DOWNLOADABLE RESOURCES

The resources in this book are available for you
as a digital download!

Please visit **15minutefocusseries.com** and click this book
cover on the page. Once you've clicked the book cover,
a prompt will ask you for a code to unlock the activities.

Please enter code:

Selfharm334

EMOTION REGULATION

What is it and how do we do it?

What is Emotion Regulation?

"Emotion Regulation" is a term generally used to describe a person's ability to effectively manage and respond to an emotional experience. many people unconsciously use emotion regulation strategies to cope with difficult situations throughout the day.

Common **Healthy** Emotion Regulation Strategies

Talking with Friends

Exercizing

Meditation

Common **Unhealthy** Emotion Regulation Strategies

Self-Injury

Substance Abuse

Excessive Social Media Use

"Vicious Cycle"

Situation
(What triggers the problem)
E.g. criticized at work

My Thoughts
(What goes through my head?)
"I'm not good enough."

My Body's Physical Reaction
Feel tired, loss of appetite

My Emotions
(How do I feel?)
Worthless, anxious

My Behavior
(What do I do?)
Isolate myself, avoid contact with others

Emotion Dysregulation

- Inability to regularly use healthy strategies to diffuse or moderate negative emotions
- It is the interpretation of the emotion that tends to stir up feelings and a sense of not being able to tolerate them

Breaking the Cycle

- Learning how to understand and work with the relationships between thoughts, feelings, and behaviors
- Pay attention to the way the thought-emotion-behavior realtionship works for each of us

Male and Female Differences in Emotion Regulation

♂ **VS.** ♀

- Experience both positive and negative emotions more intensely
- Greater difficulties with emotion regulation skills
- More difficulty controlling ruminating behaviors
- More prone to "reflection"

- Experience both positive and negative emotions less intensely
- Less difficulties with emotion regulation skills

Tips for Regulating Emotions

Take Care of Your Physical Needs

Engage in Activities that Build a Sense of Achievement

Changing Thoughts is Easier than Changing Feelings

- Good night's rest
- Eat healthy
- Exercise your body

- Do one positive thing every day
- Pay more attention to the positive events in our lives

- Evaluate what you are thinkingthat is causing the emotion
- What is it that's really pushing my buttons here?

For More Resources

Cornell Research Program on Self-Injury and Recovery
www.selfinjury.bctr.cornell.edu

Youth Risk and Opportunity Lab
www.yrocornell.com

Emotion Regulation Information Brief
Rolston, A., & Lloyd-Richardson, E.
What is emotion regulation and how do we do it?
Cornell Research Program in Self-Injury and Recovery

Courtesy of The National Institute of Mental Health Information Resource Center.
Visit www.nimh.nih.gov for more information.

5 Action Steps for Helping Someone in Emotional Pain

In 2018, suicide claimed the lives of more than **48,000 people** in the United States, according to the Centers for Disease Control and Prevention (CDC). Suicide affects people of all ages, genders, races, and ethnicities.

Suicide is complicated and tragic, but it can be preventable. **Knowing the warning signs for suicide and how to get help can help save lives.**

Here are 5 steps you can take to #BeThe1To help someone in emotional pain:

1. ASK:
"Are you thinking about killing yourself?" It's not an easy question but studies show that asking at-risk individuals if they are suicidal does not increase suicides or suicidal thoughts.

2. KEEP THEM SAFE:
Reducing a suicidal person's access to highly lethal items or places is an important part of suicide prevention. While this is not always easy, asking if the at-risk person has a plan and removing or disabling the lethal means can make a difference.

3. BE THERE:
Listen carefully and learn what the individual is thinking and feeling. Research suggests acknowledging and talking about suicide may in fact reduce rather than increase suicidal thoughts.

4. HELP THEM CONNECT:
Save the National Suicide Prevention Lifeline number **(1-800-273-TALK)** and the Crisis Text Line **(741741)** in your phone so they're there if you need them. You can also help make a connection with a trusted individual like a family member, friend, spiritual advisor, or mental health professional.

5. STAY CONNECTED:
Staying in touch after a crisis or after being discharged from care can make a difference. Studies have shown the number of suicide deaths goes down when someone follows up with the at-risk person.

For more information on suicide prevention:
www.nimh.nih.gov/suicideprevention
www.bethe1to.com

National Institute of Mental Health

NIMH Identifier No. OM 20-4315
Revised 2020

Courtesy of The National Institute of Mental Health Information Resource Center.
Visit www.nimh.nih.gov for more information.

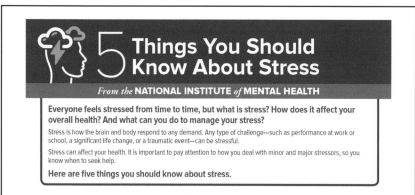

5 Things You Should Know About Stress

From the NATIONAL INSTITUTE of MENTAL HEALTH

Everyone feels stressed from time to time, but what is stress? How does it affect your overall health? And what can you do to manage your stress?

Stress is how the brain and body respond to any demand. Any type of challenge—such as performance at work or school, a significant life change, or a traumatic event—can be stressful.

Stress can affect your health. It is important to pay attention to how you deal with minor and major stressors, so you know when to seek help.

Here are five things you should know about stress.

1. Stress affects everyone.

Everyone experiences stress from time to time. There are different types of stress—all of which carry physical and mental health risks. A stressor may be a one-time or short-term occurrence, or it can happen repeatedly over a long time. Some people may cope with stress more effectively and recover from stressful events more quickly than others.

Examples of stress include:

- Routine stress related to the pressures of school, work, family, and other daily responsibilities.
- Stress brought about by a sudden negative change, such as losing a job, divorce, or illness.
- Traumatic stress experienced during an event such as a major accident, war, assault, or natural disaster where people may be in danger of being seriously hurt or killed. People who experience traumatic stress may have very distressing temporary emotional and physical symptoms, but most recover naturally soon after. Read more about Coping With Traumatic Events (www.nimh.nih.gov/copingwithtrauma).

2. Not all stress is bad.

In a dangerous situation, stress signals the body to prepare to face a threat or flee to safety. In these situations, your pulse quickens, you breathe faster, your muscles tense, and your brain uses more oxygen and increases activity—all functions aimed at survival and in response to stress. In non-life-threatening situations, stress can motivate people, such as when they need to take a test or interview for a new job.

3. Long-term stress can harm your health.

Coping with the impact of chronic stress can be challenging. Because the source of long-term stress is more constant than acute stress, the body never receives a clear signal to return to normal functioning. With chronic stress, those same lifesaving reactions in the body can disturb the immune, digestive, cardiovascular, sleep, and reproductive systems. Some people may experience mainly digestive symptoms, while others may have headaches, sleeplessness, sadness, anger, or irritability.

Over time, continued strain on your body from stress may contribute to serious health problems, such as heart disease, high blood pressure, diabetes, and other illnesses, including mental disorders such as depression (www.nimh.nih.gov/depression) or anxiety (www.nimh.nih.gov/anxietydisorders).

Courtesy of The National Institute of Mental Health Information Resource Center.
Visit www.nimh.nih.gov for more information.

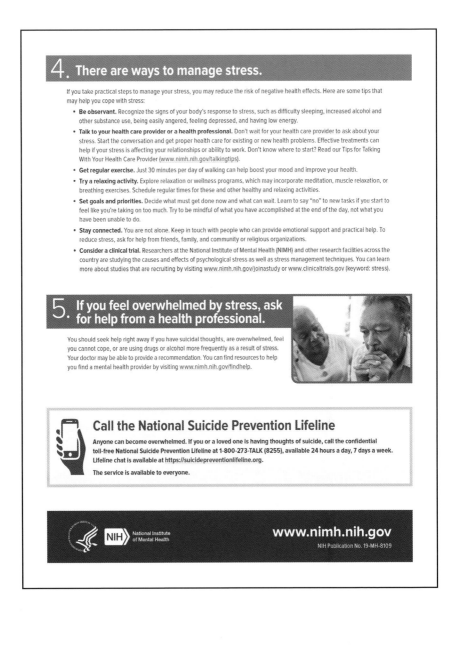

4. There are ways to manage stress.

If you take practical steps to manage your stress, you may reduce the risk of negative health effects. Here are some tips that may help you cope with stress:

- **Be observant.** Recognize the signs of your body's response to stress, such as difficulty sleeping, increased alcohol and other substance use, being easily angered, feeling depressed, and having low energy.
- **Talk to your health care provider or a health professional.** Don't wait for your health care provider to ask about your stress. Start the conversation and get proper health care for existing or new health problems. Effective treatments can help if your stress is affecting your relationships or ability to work. Don't know where to start? Read our Tips for Talking With Your Health Care Provider (www.nimh.nih.gov/talkingtips).
- **Get regular exercise.** Just 30 minutes per day of walking can help boost your mood and improve your health.
- **Try a relaxing activity.** Explore relaxation or wellness programs, which may incorporate meditation, muscle relaxation, or breathing exercises. Schedule regular times for these and other healthy and relaxing activities.
- **Set goals and priorities.** Decide what must get done now and what can wait. Learn to say "no" to new tasks if you start to feel like you're taking on too much. Try to be mindful of what you have accomplished at the end of the day, not what you have been unable to do.
- **Stay connected.** You are not alone. Keep in touch with people who can provide emotional support and practical help. To reduce stress, ask for help from friends, family, and community or religious organizations.
- **Consider a clinical trial.** Researchers at the National Institute of Mental Health (NIMH) and other research facilities across the country are studying the causes and effects of psychological stress as well as stress management techniques. You can learn more about studies that are recruiting by visiting www.nimh.nih.gov/joinastudy or www.clinicaltrials.gov (keyword: stress).

5. If you feel overwhelmed by stress, ask for help from a health professional.

You should seek help right away if you have suicidal thoughts, are overwhelmed, feel you cannot cope, or are using drugs or alcohol more frequently as a result of stress. Your doctor may be able to provide a recommendation. You can find resources to help you find a mental health provider by visiting www.nimh.nih.gov/findhelp.

Call the National Suicide Prevention Lifeline

Anyone can become overwhelmed. If you or a loved one is having thoughts of suicide, call the confidential toll-free National Suicide Prevention Lifeline at 1-800-273-TALK (8255), available 24 hours a day, 7 days a week. Lifeline chat is available at https://suicidepreventionlifeline.org.

The service is available to everyone.

NIH National Institute of Mental Health

www.nimh.nih.gov
NIH Publication No. 19-MH-8109

Courtesy of The National Institute of Mental Health Information Resource Center.
Visit www.nimh.nih.gov for more information.

STRESS CATCHER
CATCH SOME GREAT COPING STRATEGIES AND SKILLS FOR MANAGING STRESS
From the NATIONAL INSTITUTE *of* MENTAL HEALTH

Life can get challenging sometimes, and it's important for kids (and adults!) to develop strategies for coping with stress or anxiety. This stress catcher "fortune teller" offers some strategies children can practice and use to help manage stress and other difficult emotions.

Follow the instructions to create a fun and interactive way for children to practice coping strategies.

CREATE YOUR STRESS CATCHER

STEP 1. Color the stress catcher (on page 2), and cut out the square.

STEP 2. Place the stress catcher face down. Fold each corner to the opposite corner, and then unfold to create two diagonal creases in the square.

STEP 3. Fold each corner toward the center of the square so that the numbers and colors are facing you. Turn over the square, and again fold each corner into the center so that the color names are visible.

STEP 4. Fold the square in half so that the color names are touching, and the numbers are on the outside. Now open it and fold it in half the other way.

STEP 5. Insert your thumb and first finger of each hand (pinching motion) under the number flaps.

STEP 6. Close the stress catcher so only the numbers show.

USE YOUR STRESS CATCHER

1. Pick a number, and open and close the stress catcher that number of times.
2. Next, pick a color and spell out the color name, opening and closing the stress catcher for each letter.
3. Then pick a color that is visible and open that flap.
4. Read what it says, and practice the coping strategy.
5. This game can be played with one or two players and is a way to practice coping strategies.

ADDITIONAL RESOURCES

5 Things You Should Know About Stress
www.nimh.nih.gov/stress

The Teen Brain: 7 Things to Know
www.nimh.nih.gov/teenbrain

5 Action Steps for Helping Someone in Emotional Pain
www.nimh.nih.gov/health/publications/5-action-steps-for-helping-someone-in-emotional-pain

National Suicide Prevention Lifeline
www.suicidepreventionlifeline.org
1-800-273-TALK (8255) for free 24-hour help

Crisis Text Line
www.crisistextline.org
Text HELLO to 741741 for free 24-hour help

For more information about mental health, visit the NIMH website at **www.nimh.nih.gov**. For information on a wide variety of health topics, visit the National Library of Medicine's MedlinePlus service at **https://medlineplus.gov**.

NIH> National Institute of Mental Health

www.nimh.nih.gov
NIH Publication No. 20-MH-8121

Courtesy of The National Institute of Mental Health Information Resource Center.
Visit www.nimh.nih.gov for more information.

8 7 ORANGE YELLOW 9 5

RED Tell yourself the facts, and don't focus on the worst-case scenario. Laugh! Find something funny! Listen to or play music. Imagine a beautiful and peaceful place. GREEN

Talk it out With a trusted adult or friend. Exercise! Play outside. Ride a bike, dance, or take a walk. Take a few deep breaths. Breathe in through your nose and out through your mouth. Write down everything you are feeling. BLUE

BROWN 1 2 PINK PURPLE 3 4

REPLACEMENT STRATEGIES

Reach Out to Others

- Phone a friend.
- Call 1-800-DONT-CUT.
- Go out and be around people.

Express Yourself

- Write down your feelings in a diary.
- Cry as a way to express your sadness or frustration.
- Draw or color.

Keep Busy

- Play a game.
- Listen to music.
- Read.
- Take a shower.
- Open a dictionary and learn new words.
- Do homework.
- Cook.
- Dig in the garden.
- Clean.
- Watch a feel-good movie.

Do Something Mindful

- Count down slowly from 10 to 0.
- Breathe slowly, in through the nose and out through the mouth.
- Focus on objects around you and thinking about how they look, sound, smell, taste, and feel.
- Do yoga.
- Meditate.
- Learn breathing exercises to aid relaxation.
- Concentrate on something that makes you happy: good friends, good times, laughter, etc.

Release Your Frustrations

- Throw ice cubes at a brick wall.
- Throw eggs in the shower.
- Rip apart an old magazine or phone book.
- Smash fruit with a bat or hammer..
- Throw darts.
- Punch pillows.
- Scream into a pillow.
- Slam doors.
- Yell or sing at the top of your lungs.
- Exercise.

Express Pain and Intense Emotions

- Paint, draw, or scribble on a big piece of paper with red ink or paint.
- Write in a journal to express your feelings.
- Compose a poem or song to say what you feel.
- Write down any negative feelings and then rip the paper up.
- Listen to music that expresses what you're feeling.

Feel Guilty or Deserve Punishment

- List as many good things about yourself as you can.
- Read something good that someone has written about you.
- Talk to someone who cares about you.
- Do something nice for someone else.
- Remember when you've done something good.
- Think about why you feel guilty and how you might be able to change it.

Feel Sad or Depressed

- Take a bath or hot shower.
- Pet or cuddle a dog or cat.
- Wrap yourself in a warm/weighted blanket.
- Massage your neck, hands, and feet.
- Listen to calming music.
- Do something slow and soothing.
- Give yourself a present.
- Hug a loved one.
- Make a list of things that make you happy.
- Do something nice for someone else.
- Smell sweet-smelling essential oils.
- Smooth lotion onto the parts of yourself you want to hurt.
- Call a friend.
- Watch TV or read.

Feel Numb or Disconnected

- Call a friend (you don't have to talk about self-harm).
- Take a cold shower or bath.
- Hold an ice cube in the crook of your arm or leg.
- Chew something with a very strong taste, like chili peppers, peppermint, ginger root, or a grapefruit peel.
- Go online to a self-help website, chat room, or message board.
- Squeeze ice.
- List the many uses for a random object. (For example, what are all the things you can do with a twist tie?)
- Put a finger into a frozen food (like ice cream).
- Slap a tabletop hard.
- Stomp your feet on the ground.
- Focus on how it feels to breathe. Notice the way your chest and stomach move with each breath.

Release Anger or Tension

- Exercise vigorously (run, dance, jump rope, or hit a punching bag).
- Punch a cushion or mattress or scream into your pillow.
- Squeeze a stress ball or squish Play-Doh or clay.
- Rip something up (sheets of paper, a magazine).
- Make some noise (play an instrument, bang on pots and pans).
- Slash an empty plastic soda bottle or a piece of heavy cardboard or an old shirt or sock.
- Squeeze ice.
- Do something that will give you a sharp sensation, like eating lemon.
- Make a soft cloth doll to represent the things you are angry at. Cut and tear it instead of yourself.
- Flatten aluminum cans for recycling, seeing how fast you can go.
- Pick up a stick and hit a tree.
- Use a pillow to hit a wall, pillow-fight style.
- On a sketch or photo of yourself, mark in red ink what you want to do. Cut and tear the picture.
- Make clay models and cut or smash them.
- Clean.
- Bang pots and pans.
- Stomp around in heavy shoes.
- Play handball or tennis.

Substitutes for the Cutting Sensation

- Use a red marker pen to draw on your skin where you might usually cut.
- Rub ice cubes over your skin where you might usually cut.
- Place rubber bands on your wrists, arms, or legs, and snap them instead of cutting.
- Putting stickers on the parts of your body you want to injure.
- Drawing slashing lines on paper.
- Paint on your skin with red watercolor or tempera paint.
- Drawing on the areas you want to cut using ice that you've made by dropping six or seven drops of red food color into each of the ice-cube tray wells.

Courtesy of The Cornell Research Program on Self-Injury and Recovery.
Visit www.cornell.edu for more information.

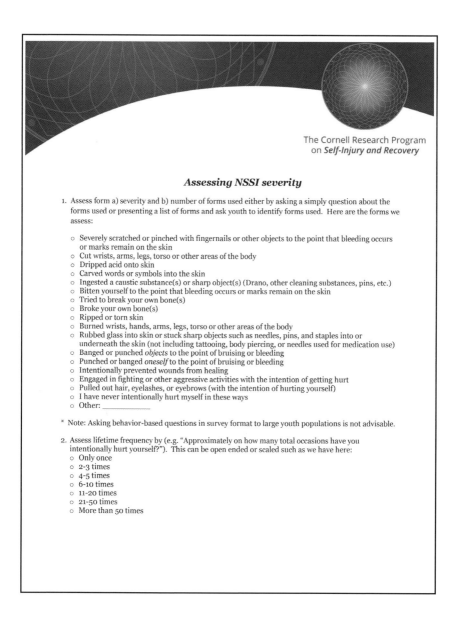

The Cornell Research Program
on *Self-Injury and Recovery*

Assessing NSSI severity

1. Assess form a) severity and b) number of forms used either by asking a simply question about the forms used or presenting a list of forms and ask youth to identify forms used. Here are the forms we assess:

   - Severely scratched or pinched with fingernails or other objects to the point that bleeding occurs or marks remain on the skin
   - Cut wrists, arms, legs, torso or other areas of the body
   - Dripped acid onto skin
   - Carved words or symbols into the skin
   - Ingested a caustic substance(s) or sharp object(s) (Drano, other cleaning substances, pins, etc.)
   - Bitten yourself to the point that bleeding occurs or marks remain on the skin
   - Tried to break your own bone(s)
   - Broke your own bone(s)
   - Ripped or torn skin
   - Burned wrists, hands, arms, legs, torso or other areas of the body
   - Rubbed glass into skin or stuck sharp objects such as needles, pins, and staples into or underneath the skin (not including tattooing, body piercing, or needles used for medication use)
   - Banged or punched *objects* to the point of bruising or bleeding
   - Punched or banged *oneself* to the point of bruising or bleeding
   - Intentionally prevented wounds from healing
   - Engaged in fighting or other aggressive activities with the intention of getting hurt
   - Pulled out hair, eyelashes, or eyebrows (with the intention of hurting yourself)
   - I have never intentionally hurt myself in these ways
   - Other: _____

   * Note: Asking behavior-based questions in survey format to large youth populations is not advisable.

2. Assess lifetime frequency by (e.g. "Approximately on how many total occasions have you intentionally hurt yourself?"). This can be open ended or scaled such as we have here:
   - Only once
   - 2-3 times
   - 4-5 times
   - 6-10 times
   - 11-20 times
   - 21-50 times
   - More than 50 times

Courtesy of The Cornell Research Program on Self-Injury and Recovery.
Visit www.cornell.edu for more information.

Characteristics of high severity class:

- Greater than 11 lifetime incidents
- Use more than 2 forms (often more than 3 forms)
- Use at least one form likely to cause severe tissue damage: cutting or carving the body, burning areas of the body, breaking bones, dripping acid onto skin, and ingesting a caustic substance(s) or sharp object(s)
- Our study found that 42.7% of those who reported SI fell into this class and 71% of these were female.
- This class is more likely than no-SIers to report: suicidality, disordered eating, struggling with other mental health challenges / disorders, and to history of sexual, emotional and/or physical trauma. They are also more likely to have been in therapy or to clearly need therapy.
- Compared to the other SI groups, they are more likely to have friends who self-injure, to show strong habituation (addiction tendencies), and to have hurt themselves more severely than intended.

Characteristics of moderate severity class:

- 2-10 lifetime incidents
- 2-3 forms
- use at least one form likely to cause bruising or light tissue damage such as punching or banging oneself or other objects (with the express intention of hurting the self), sticking sharp objects into the skin (not including tattooing, body piercing, or needles used for medication use), and self-bruising.
- Our study showed that 38% of those who report SI fell into this group and 60% of this group were men
- More likely than non-SIers to report suicidality, disordered eating, emotional abuse, & history of therapy.

Characteristics of low severity class:

- Majority report fewer than 10 lifetime incidents (though about 25% report up to 50 lifetime incidents)
- Vast majority use only one form
- All forms use likely to cause superficial tissue damage such as scratching or pinching to the point that bleeding occurs or marks remain on the skin; intentionally preventing wounds from healing
- Our study showed that 15% of those reporting SI fell into this category; 72% female
- More likely than non-SIers to report suicidality, disordered eating, emotional abuse, & history of therapy (about the same magnitude of risk as moderate lethality class)

Taken from:

Whitlock, J.L., Exner-Cortens, D. & Purington, A. (under review). Validity and reliability of the non-suicidal self-injury assessment test (NSSI-AT).

Whitlock, J.L., Muehlenkamp, J., Eckenrode, J. (2008). Variation in non-suicidal self-injury: Identification of latent classes in a community population of young adults. *Journal of Clinical Child and Adolescent Psychology.* 37(4). 725-735.

Courtesy of The National Institute of Mental Health Information Resource Center.
Visit www.nimh.nih.gov for more information.

NIMH TOOLKIT

asQ
Ask Suicide-Screening Questions

Suicide Risk **Screening Tool**

Ask the patient:

1. In the past few weeks, have you wished you were dead? ○ Yes ○ No

2. In the past few weeks, have you felt that you or your family would be better off if you were dead? ○ Yes ○ No

3. In the past week, have you been having thoughts about killing yourself? ○ Yes ○ No

4. Have you ever tried to kill yourself? ○ Yes ○ No

   If yes, how? _____

   _____

   _____

   When? _____

   _____

If the patient answers Yes to any of the above, ask the following acuity question:

5. Are you having thoughts of killing yourself right now? ○ Yes ○ No

   If yes, please describe: _____

Next steps:

- If patient answers "No" to all questions 1 through 4, screening is complete (not necessary to ask question #5). No intervention is necessary (*Note: Clinical judgment can always override a negative screen).

- If patient answers "Yes" to any of questions 1 through 4, or refuses to answer, they are considered a **positive screen**. Ask question #5 to assess acuity:

  ☐ "Yes" to question #5 = **acute positive screen** (imminent risk identified)
    - **Patient requires a STAT safety/full mental health evaluation.** Patient cannot leave until evaluated for safety.
    - Keep patient in sight. Remove all dangerous objects from room. Alert physician or clinician responsible for patient's care.

  ☐ "No" to question #5 = **non-acute positive screen** (potential risk identified)
    - **Patient requires a brief suicide safety assessment to determine if a full mental health evaluation is needed.** Patient cannot leave until evaluated for safety.
    - Alert physician or clinician responsible for patient's care.

Provide resources to all patients

- 24/7 National Suicide Prevention Lifeline 1-800-273-TALK (8255) En Español: 1-888-628-9454
- 24/7 Crisis Text Line: Text "HOME" to 741-741

asQ Suicide Risk Screening Toolkit   NATIONAL INSTITUTE OF MENTAL HEALTH (NIMH)   NIH   7/1/2020

Courtesy of The Cornell Research Program on Self-Injury and Recovery.
Visit www.cornell.edu for more information.

Cornell Research Program on
Self-Injury and Recovery

BY MIRANDA SWEET & JANIS WHITLOCK

Information for parents
What you need to know about self-injury.

Who is this for?

Parents of those dealing with self-injury

What is included?

How do you know if your child is self-injuring?

Dealing with feelings about this discovery

Talking to your child about his/her self-injury

What to avoid saying to your child

Activities to help others manage their urges

Self-injury and your relationship with your child

Self-injury and the home environment

Finding treatment

Supporting your child while he/she is getting help

Discovering Self-Injury

How do I know if my child is self-injuring?

Many adolescents who self-injure do so in secrecy and this secrecy is often the clearest red flag that something is wrong. Although it is normal for adolescents to pull away from parents during times of high involvement with friends or stress, it is *not* normal for adolescents to be withdrawn, physically and emotionally, for long periods of time. It is also important to note that not all people who self-injure become distant and withdrawn — youth who put on a happy face, even when they do not feel happy, may also be at risk for self-injury or other negative coping behaviors. Some other signs include:

- Cut or burn marks on arms, legs, abdomen
- Discovery of hidden razors, knives, other sharp objects and rubber bands (which may be used to increase blood flow or numb the area)
- Spending long periods of time alone, particularly in the bathroom or bedroom
- Wearing clothing inappropriate for the weather, such as long sleeves or pants in hot weather

What might I feel when I learn that my child is self-injuring, and how do I deal with these feelings?

If you learn your child is self-injuring, you are likely to experience a range of emotions, from shock or anger, to sadness or guilt. All of these are valid feelings.

- **Shock and denial**
  Because self-injury is a secretive behavior, it may be shocking to learn that your child is intentionally hurting him or herself; however, to deny the behavior is to deny your child's emotional distress.
- **Anger and frustration**
  You may feel angry or frustrated that your child has possibly lied to you about his/her injuries or because you see the behavior as pointless or because it is out of your control.
  As one parent said, "There is a frustration in terms of that little voice in the back of your mind that is saying 'just stop it!' It's very hard, I think knowing more about the condition and about the underlying factors makes it easier to push that little voice away."[1]

  …but remember that *you can never control another person's behavior,* even your child's, and trying to do this does not make things better.
- **Empathy, sympathy and sadness**
  Though empathy helps you to understand your child's situation, sympathy and sadness can sometimes be condescending because they imply that your child needs to be pitied. These feelings may also hinder your ability to understand the behavior.
- **Guilt**
  You may feel as if you did not offer enough love and attention to your child. However, though your actions can influence your child's behavior, you do not *cause* their self-injury.

General stress-relieving techniques may help with managing these difficult emotions. For specific suggestions, visit http://www.selfinjury.bctr.cornell.edu/factsheet_coping_alternatives.asp

FYI

PAGE 1 OF 7

Courtesy of The Cornell Research Program on Self-Injury and Recovery.
Visit www.cornell.edu for more information.

Opening the Lines of Communication

How should I talk to my child about his/her self-injury?

- Address the issue **as soon as possible.** Don't presume that your child will simply "outgrow" the behavior and that it will go away on its own. (Though keep in mind this can and does happen for some young people–some do mention "outgrowing" their self-injury. This typically occurs because they learn more adaptive ways of coping).
- Try to **use your concern** in a constructive way, by helping your child realize the impact of his/her self-injury on themselves and others.

- It is most important to **validate your child's feelings.** Remember that this is different from validating the behavior.
  - Parents must first make eye contact and be respectful listeners before offering their opinion
  - Speak in calm and comforting tones
  - Offer reassurance
  - Consider what was helpful to you as an adolescent when experiencing emotional distress
- If your child does not want to talk, **do not pressure** him/her. Self-injury is a very emotional subject and the behavior itself is often an indication that your child has difficulty verbalizing his/her emotions.

What are some helpful questions I can ask my child to better understand his/her self-injury?[2]

Recognize that direct questions may feel invasive and frightening at first—particularly when coming from someone known and cared for, like you. It is most productive to focus first on helping your child to acknowledge the problem and the need for help. Here are some examples of what you might say:

- "How do you feel before you self-injure? How do you feel after you self-injure?" Retrace the steps leading up to an incident of self-injury—the events, thoughts, and feelings which led to it.
- "How does self-injury help you feel better?"
- "What is it like for you to talk with me about hurting yourself?"

- "Is there anything that is really stressing you out right now that I can help you with?"
- "Is there anything missing in our relationship, that if it were present, would make a difference?"
- "If you don't wish to talk to me about this now, I understand. I just want you to know that I am here for you when you decide you are ready to talk. Is it okay if I check in with you about this or would you prefer to come to me?"

> "...internal pain wasn't real and wasn't something you that you could heal. And if you make it external, it's real, you can see it... I needed to have it be in a place other than inside me."
> —Interviewee

What are some things I should AVOID saying or doing?

The following behaviors can actually increase your child's self-injury behaviors:[3]
- Yelling
- Lecturing
- Put downs
- Harsh and lengthy punishments
- Invasions of privacy (i.e., going through your child's bedroom without his/her presence)
- Ultimatums
- Threats

Avoid power struggles. You cannot control another person's behavior and demanding that your loved one stop self-injuring is generally unproductive.

The following statements are examples of **unhelpful** things to say:
- "I know how you feel." This can make your child feel as if their problems are trivialized.
- "How can you be so crazy to do this to yourself?"
- "You are doing this to make me feel guilty."

Take your child seriously. One individual who struggles with self-injury described her disclosure to her parents in the following way: "They freaked and made me promise not to do it again. I said yes just to make them feel better though. That settled everything for them. I felt hurt that they did not take me serious[ly] and get me help."[4]

Courtesy of The Cornell Research Program on Self-Injury and Recovery.
Visit www.cornell.edu for more information.

How do I know if I am doing or saying the right thing?

- Parents need to ask for feedback from their child about how well they are doing their job as parents.
  - This demonstrates that they are truly engaged in improving and strengthening their relationship with their child.
  - Parents can identify specifically what they can do to contribute to their child's success.

Are there any activities I can complete with my child to help them manage their urges to self-injure?

The Nillumbik Community Health Service has developed an activity for identifying who can be helpers and specifically how they can help. There is a worksheet to fill in who is available at different times throughout the day for support. To link to this worksheet, see http://www.nchs.org.au/Docs/SelfHarm_StuInfoPack.pdf. If your child has already developed a list of effective coping strategies for managing distress (for more on this, see http://www.selfinjury.bctr.cornell.edu/factsheet_coping_alternatives.asp), this information can be put together to create a "help card," which includes your child's top coping strategies and phone numbers of support people, and can be easily carried around in a wallet for whenever the need for support may arise. Go to Appendix M of http://www.sfys.infoxchange.net.au/resources/public/items/2004/12/00131-upload-00001.doc to link to the help card activity.

> *"Parents, there is hope. If you are facing some of the difficulties we have... don't give up.*
> *You need to fight; many teachers, doctors and counselors may not have the knowledge or ability*
> *to help — keep fighting. Don't give up; there can be a bright light at the end of the tunnel."*
> — Parent collaborators on CRPSIR team

FYI   To read more about the personal experiences of these parents, see
http://www.selfinjury.bctr.cornell.edu/factsheet_personal_stories.asp

> *"I stopped because I developed a sense of worth and, to some extent, love for*
> *myself. I also have come to understand that it is painful for those I love to know*
> *I cut myself, so I have partially stopped so I would not hurt them. I've learned*
> *better coping strategies as well."*
> — Survey Participant

Cornell Research Program on Self-Injury and Recovery

PAGE 3 OF 7

Courtesy of The Cornell Research Program on Self-Injury and Recovery.
Visit www.cornell.edu for more information.

Understanding the Role of Relationships

Is my child's self-injury my fault?

No, no person causes another person to act in a certain way. Like most negative behaviors, however, self-injury is often a result of two things. That is, a person's belief that he or she cannot handle the stress they feel, and that self-injury is a good way to deal with stress. A history of strained relations with parents and/or peers, high emotional sensitivity, and low ability to manage emotion all contribute to these beliefs. This can lead to the use of self-injury in order to cope. Parent-child relationships strongly influence a child's (and parents') emotional state. Youth with high emotion sensitivity and few emotion management skills may be particularly sensitive to stressful dynamics within the relationship, especially if they

continue for a long time. For this reason, negative parent-child interactions are often powerful triggers for self-injury. However, they are also powerful in aiding recovery and, most importantly, to the development of positive coping skills. Parents who are willing to understand the powerful role they play, to directly confront painful dynamics within the family, to be fully present for their child, and to help their child see that he or she has a choice in how they cope with life challenges, will be allies in the recovery process. Parents who try to fix their child by taking responsibility for their child's problems may actually make recovery more difficult.

How might my relationship with my child affect his/her self-injury?[2]

- Extremes in the quality of the parents' attachment (such as a lack of boundaries or too much emotional distance, or extreme overprotective or hovering behavior) are common in today's society.
  - Many adolescents who struggle with self-injury report that their parents are either unavailable to them for emotional support or invalidate their feelings, which has led them to believe that they are worthless or not worthy of being loved.
  - Alternatively, parents who cope *for* their kids by seeking to closely control their behavior, attitudes and/or choices run the risk of undermining their children's capacity to develop effective ways of handling stress and adversity.

- The importance of secure attachments:
  - Adolescents who feel secure and positive attachment bonds with their parents are less likely to gravitate to negative peer groups or be victims of peer pressure.
  - Resilient children and adolescents, that is, those who have the ability to quickly rebound from painful life events, say that their secure attachments with their parents or key caretakers have a significant influence on their ability to cope effectively.

  According to Selekman (2006), mothers tend to average 8 minutes a day in conversation with their adolescents. Fathers spend only 3 minutes.

How might my child's peer relationships affect his or her self-injury?

If children feel as if their needs are not being met at home, they may turn to a so-called "second family," such as a street gang or a negative peer group. This is particularly likely to happen if parents work long hours. Children may turn to this second family because they feel that their parents are too busy to spend time with them. What is particularly troubling

is that self-injury may sometimes be a part of the culture of the second family. For example, one adolescent described how she and her friends would play a game called "chicken," in which the participants superficially wounded themselves, and the winner was the individual who could inflict the most cuts without "chickening out."[3]

> "I think probably one of the most difficult things for people who don't self injure to understand, what I've been asked time and time again, is why do you do it? It's so many years of depression behind it. You can't answer 'I cut because of this and this and this." And also, how physically addictive it is. It feels so necessary and so right."
> — Interviewee

Cornell Research Program on Self-Injury and Recovery

Courtesy of The Cornell Research Program on Self-Injury and Recovery.
Visit www.cornell.edu for more information.

Improving the Home Environment

What aspects of the home environment might be affecting my child's self-injury?[6]

- **Repression and/or mismanagement of emotion**
  Self-injury is most commonly understood as an emotion regulation technique. This suggests that individuals who practice it have difficulty regulating emotional states healthfully. In some cases, this tendency is a result of a family history of repressing or mismanaging emotion, such as when family members either do not know how to constructively express negative feelings like anger or fear, or when they withhold demonstrations of love and tenderness with their children.

- **Family secrets**
  All families have stories to tell, not all of which are easy to share or hear. When a child or adolescent is directly involved with negative events occurring within the family and then told or chooses not to share what is happening with someone he or she trusts, he/she may suffer—psychologically and physically. Depression, anxiety, and a variety of self-injurious behaviors are all potential consequences of keeping family secrets.

How can I foster a protective home environment?

- Model healthy ways of managing stress.
- Keep lines of communication and exchange open.
- Emphasize and uphold the importance of family time.
- Expect that your child will contribute to the family's chores and responsibilities.
- Set limits and consistently enforce consequences when these are violated. Consider positive consequences, such as working in a soup kitchen or other community service.
- Respect the development of your child's individuality.
- Provide firm guidelines around technology usage. Many individuals who struggle with self-injury report spending several hours a day interacting on the Internet with other self-injurers (particularly via message boards—many of which are not regulated) while engaging in their harming behaviors. Though the majority of the information shared is supportive, some of these sites actually encourage self-injury and even share harming techniques.
- Do not take your child's self-injury tools away. This suggestion is often surprising to parents. However, if your child has the strong urge to injure him/herself,

he/she will find a way (and it may not be as safe). Also, using the same tools is sometimes part of the ritual of self-injury, so the panic of losing this aspect of control can actually trigger more harming episodes.
- Remember that respect is a two-way street.
  – Keep the atmosphere at home inviting, positive, and upbeat.
  – Positive emotion promotes resiliency and serves as a protective measure.
- Practice using positive coping skills together.
- Avoid over-scheduling your child and putting too much pressure on him or her to perform.
- Don't expect a quick fix. There will be setbacks along the way to recovery, and a slip does not mean that your child is not making progress; these are common during stages of change. See the next page for more information about the **five stages of change**, which has been applied to a broad range of behaviors.

"Easy access to a virtual subculture of like-minded others may reinforce the behavior for a much larger number of youth."
—Janis Whitlock, Ph.D., MPH

Cornell Research Program on Self-Injury and Recovery

Courtesy of The Cornell Research Program on Self-Injury and Recovery.
Visit www.cornell.edu for more information.

FIVE STAGES OF CHANGE

1 **Precontemplation:** The individual is not seriously thinking about changing his/her behavior and may not even consider that he/she has a problem. For example, your child may defend the benefits of his/her self-injury and not acknowledge the negative consequences of harming him/herself.

2 **Contemplation:** The individual is thinking more about the behavior and the negative aspects of continuing to practice it. Though the individual is more open to the possibility of changing, he/she is often ambivalent about it. For example, your child may be considering the benefits of decreasing his/her self-injury, but may wonder whether it is worth it to give up the behavior.

3 **Preparation:** The individual has made a commitment to change his/her behavior. He/she may research treatment options and consider the lifestyle changes that will have to be made. For example, your child may look for a support group to plan for the difficulties of decreasing his/her self-injury.

4 **Action:** The individual has confidence in his/her ability to change and is taking active steps. For example, your child might begin practicing **alternative coping mechanisms** (see http://www.selfinjury.bctr.cornell.edu/factsheet_coping_alternatives.asp), like journaling, rather than engaging in self-injury. Unfortunately, this is also the stage where the individual is most vulnerable to a relapse, because learning new techniques for managing your emotions is a gradual learning process. Support is vital to this stage—this is where you come in!

5 **Maintenance:** The individual is working to maintain the changes he/she has made. He/she is aware of triggers and how these may affect his/her goals. For example, if your child knows that studying for an upcoming calculus test sometimes triggers the urge to self-injure, he/she might join a study group to reduce the likelihood of self-injuring.

> "Therapy helped me deal with other issues which in turn helped me stop hurting myself. Hurting my self was not the central issue in my therapy sessions... I hurt myself because I was depressed, so we worked on getting the depression under control and then the intentional hurting myself ceased because not only was I no longer depressed but I knew myself better to know the correct way FOR ME to control problems that I would have later."
> — Survey Participant

Finding Treatment

Know that seeking help for someone, particularly a youth, is a sign of love, not betrayal. You can provide some choices about where to go and who to see. You can also include him/her in decisions about how and what to tell other family members if that becomes a necessity.

How can I find a therapist for my child?[7]

The S.A.F.E. Alternatives website (http://www.selfinjury.com) provides a thorough overview of how to find a therapist, specifically for the treatment of self-injury. It provides suggestions for how to obtain a referral, such as asking a member of the medical field, looking in the phonebook, and researching teaching hospitals (which may have low-cost alternatives). There is also a link to a section titled "Therapist Referrals" which provides specific names and information about experienced therapists in each state. To go directly to this page of referrals, see http://www.selfinjury.com/referrals_therapistreferrals.html.

Three different therapy models are explained, including psychodymanic therapy, cognitive-behavioral therapy and supportive therapy. There are recommendations for questions to ask a therapist—and yourself—to determine whether the relationship seems to be a good match. General tips for how to get the most out of therapy and some potential difficulties to expect are included throughout the overview.

Cornell Research Program on Self-Injury and Recovery

Courtesy of The Cornell Research Program on Self-Injury and Recovery.
Visit www.cornell.edu for more information.

How can I help my child get the most out of professional help?

- **Individual Therapy**
  Avoid interrogating your child about what he/she talks about in individual therapy. The individual who self-injures is likely to need and want a measure of privacy as therapy progresses, but will also need to include significant others in some way over time. Don't expect too much in the beginning and continue working to keep lines of communication open.

- **Family therapy**
  Individuals live in families and families typically have a host of belief systems and behaviors that influence individual behavior. Increasing all family members' awareness of how the family system may inadvertently feed an individual's self-injury can be a critical step in recovery.

- **Art therapy and other visualization/multi-sensory techniques**
  Symbols and metaphors that appear in these modalities can be used to explore thoughts and feelings that may be hard to express in words. Many adolescents indicate that these therapies were most beneficial to them in their individual and family therapy sessions.

- **Group therapy**
  This may be beneficial if your child is experiencing peer difficulties and can provide additional support outside of the home.

- **Consider inpatient treatment, if necessary**
  S.A.F.E. Alternatives is currently the only inpatient treatment center for self-injury. For more information about what they offer, visit: http://www.selfinjury.com

> **FYI** Remember to take care of yourself as well! Set up your own support network. The National Alliance on Mental Health offers support groups for family members of individuals with a mental illness. http://www.nami.org/Template.cfm?Section=Your_Local_NAMI&Template=/CustomSource/AffiliateFinder.cfm to find a group in your local area.

[1] Quote from *Self-harm: management and intervention* section of BNPCA Project Report (2004).
[2] Paraphrased from the preface of Selekman (2006).
[3] List of examples from preface of Selekman (2006).
[4] Quote from *in their own words* section of the Self-Injury: A Struggle website.
[5] Example from *Self Harm: A peer-influenced behavior* section of BNPCA Project Report (2004).
http://www.stys.infoxchange.net.au/resources/public/items/2004/12/00131-upload-00001.doc
[6] Paraphrased from introduction of Selekman (2006).
[7] Summarized from *How to find a therapist* section of the SAFE Alternatives website.

References
SAFE Alternatives (2007). How to find a therapist. Retrieved from the World Wide Web:
    http://www.selfinjury.com/referrals_findatherapist.html

Selekman, Matthew D. (2006). *Working with self-harming adolescents: A collaborative strengths-based therapy approach*. New York, NY: W.W. Norton & Company.

Self-Injury: A Struggle. *In their own words*. Retrieved from the World Wide Web:
    http://self-injury.net/intheirownwords/words/how-did-people-react-when-you-told-them-you-are-a-self-injurer/16/

Wishart, Madeline. Banyule Nillumbik Primary Care Alliance (2004). *Adolescent self-harm: An exploration of the nature and prevalence in Banyule/Nillumbik.* Retrieved from Self-Injury and Related Issues Web site:
    http://www.siari.co.uk/Family_and_friends/Self_Injury_self-harm_Information_for_family_friends_and_supporters.htm

Suggested Citation
Sweet, M. & Whitlock, J.L. (2009). *Information for parents: What you need to know about self-injury*. The Fact Sheet Series, Cornell Research Program on Self-Injury and Recovery. Cornell University. Ithaca, NY

FOR MORE INFORMATION, SEE: www.selfinjury.bctr.cornell.edu

This research was supported by the Cornell University Agricultural Experiment Station federal formula funds, received from Cooperative State Research, Education and Extension Service, U.S. Department of Agriculture. Any opinions, findings, conclusions, or recommendations expressed in this publication are those of the author(s) and do not necessarily reflect the view of the U.S. Department of Agriculture.

Cornell Research Program on Self-Injury and Recovery